Journey of a Single Mother

Dasharra Bridges

Dasharra Bridges

©2016. Dasharra Bridges. All Rights Reserved.
ISBN: 978-1541112124

Published by: Kelly Publishing 2016

No part of this book may be reproduced, stored in a retrieval system or transmitted by any means without written permission from the publisher except for brief quotations in critical reviews or articles.

Unless otherwise noted Scripture quotations are from the New King James Version. Used by Permission. Scripture quotations marked NIV are from the New International Version Bible Copyright. Scripture quotations marked HCSB are from the Holman Christian Standard Bible. Scripture quotations marked AMP are from The Amplified Bible Copyright © 1954, 1958, 1962, 1964, 1965, 1987 by The Lockman Foundation. All Rights Reserved. Used by Permission.

Journey of a Single Mother

Acknowledgments

    I would like to first thank my Lord and savior Jesus Christ for showing me so much grace and mercy and changing my life completely. I would also like to say thank you to my mother, Diane and my father, Darryl for helping me raise my children. If I didn't have you in my life, I don't know how I could have got through the tough times of being a single mother. Thank you so much mommy for always lending a helping hand, if it wasn't for you and the Lord giving me strength I would have felt so alone being a single parent. I will always love and appreciate you for all that you do, from watching them while I went to school and work and always helping me with birthdays and Christmas. I am so thankful for you! To my brothers and sisters, Jermaine, Darryl, Anthony, Nikki, Betti, Joshua, and Traivon. I love you all so much and I am thankful to have all seven of you in my life. You are all the best siblings anyone can ever have! I would also like to thank the leaders that helped me grow spiritually in the Lord, Pastor Richard C Williams Jr and Elect Lady Lisa Williams of True Worship Kingdom Ministries Inc. I am so thankful that the Lord has put such an anointing on you both to help me and so many others transform our lives. You are truly blessed and you will forever hold a place in my heart. I love you both and I thank you for all that you have done for me spiritually. To my cousin, Justin Harrell (38 Spesh), you have literally been an angel in my life. Thank you so much for showing such compassion and blessing me at a time in my life when I was struggling the most. I will forever love you and remember what you have done for me and my family.

Journey of a Single Mother

To my daughter Ezaria, my princess, I love you so much words can't explain. I never knew how much I could love someone until I had you. Mommy will forever love you baby girl! To my son, Dash, my miracle baby, yes, you are my miracle. I fell in love with you the first day I looked into your precious eyes. Mommy will always love you baby boy. To all my other family, cousins, aunts, uncles, niece, nephews, grandparents, friends, I love you all! To the reader, I would first like to say thank you for taking the time out and reading my book. I hope and pray that the words in this book will bless you and change your life forever.

~Dasharra Bridges~

Table of Contents

Chapter One: **When I Lost Myself 9**

Chapter Two: **Life -Changing Decision 15**

Chapter Three: **My First Love 21**

Chapter Four: **Reality Set In 24**

Chapter Five: **Finding The Truth 30**

Chapter Six: **A Broken Promise 35**

Chapter Seven: **New Beginnings 39**

Chapter Eight: **God Heard My Cries 42**

Chapter Nine: **All I feel Is Fear 49**

Chapter Ten: **Who Can I Trust 55**

Chapter Eleven: **Answered Prayer 61**

Chapter Twelve: **Afraid of Being Judged 64**

Chapter Thirteen: **It Just Never Ends 67**

Chapter Fourteen: **The Unexpected Happens 69**

Chapter Fifteen: **For Better Or For Worse 72**

Chapter Sixteen: **My Mind Is Made Up 74**

Chapter Seventeen: **The Fallout 76**

Chapter Eighteen: **Something Wasn't Right 80**

Chapter Nineteen: **Welcome Back 85**

Chapter Twenty: **What's Done In The Dark Will Come To The Light 87**

Chapter Twenty-One: **His Lies Caught Up To Him 92**

Chapter Twenty-Two: **The Struggle 95**

Chapter Twenty-Three: **The Reveal 98**

Chapter Twenty-Four: **Rekindle The Flame 100**

Chapter Twenty-Five: **He Switched Up 103**

Chapter Twenty-Six: **Unexpected Blessing 107**

Chapter Twenty-Seven: **Left And Stressed 111**

Chapter Twenty-Eight: **Reap What You Sow 115**

Chapter Twenty-Nine: **Sacrifice 118**

Chapter Thirty: **Back Again 120**

Chapter Thirty-One: **Life Will Get Better 122**

Chapter Thirty-Two: **Leaving The Past Behind 125**

Chapter Thirty-Three: **Life Better Than Ever 127**

Dasharra Bridges

Journey of a Single Mother

Chapter One

When I Lost Myself

Why is this happening to me? I just graduated High School and I'm about to go to college. I'm not ready to throw that all away. What is everyone going to think about me now? So many thoughts were going through my mind, as I stared at that positive pregnancy test. Me pregnant, no, this can't be true. I don't know anything about being a mother. Just months ago, I was a virgin, now I'm about to have a baby! I really wish I didn't listen to my cousin Toya that night. I guess one wrong decision can change your life forever. This how it all started....

It was the summer of 2007 and my cousin Toya and I just began to start hanging out more. She was the adventurous type. She just loved to have fun. I was more conservative. I liked being home and I didn't get out much. But one night, Toya and I decided to walk to the corner store. It was a little chilly out so I put on my favorite Betty Boop Racecar Jacket, to keep me warm. We finally got to the store and bought some snacks and we began to walk back to my house. But, suddenly I heard a voice yelling, "Baby Angel, Baby Angel!" I realized that my jacket had Baby Angel written on the back, so I turned around and saw this young man running towards me. He finally catches up to me and he says "Baby Angel, my name is Terrell, can I have you?"

He was a nice-looking guy, brush cut, light skin, and he was tall. However, I just didn't want to be bothered. I honestly didn't know what to say, so he asked me again, "Can I have you?" I said, "Can you have me? No!" He was not trying to take no for an answer.

He kept on pleading his case, so I finally gave in and took his number down. Terrell and I talked on the phone a couple times and he wanted to meet with me, so we could chill. I wasn't really interested, until he said that my cousin, Toya, could come, because he had a friend named Cory she could talk to! Plus, they were only a block away, so Toya and I decided to walk over to their place to chill.

I was kind of on edge, because I don't usually go to people's houses. If anything, I would have them come to see me. But, we got there and I knocked on the door. Instantly, I got a bad vibe. Terrell opened the door and let us in. He quickly closed the door behind us and as soon as the door was closed he began to put big blocks of wood over the door, so that no one could come in or go out. Then he began to lock the door, there were so many bolted locks and he made sure he locked every one of them. As I glanced around this small house, I began to see black steel bars on all the windows, somewhat like prison windows. My heart began to race faster, looking around I can see that there is no way of getting out or getting in, unless they let you out. I don't know what I gotten myself into.

Toya and I walked in the room where Terrell and Cory were and they were listening to some rap music. They were smoking marijuana and drinking liquor. "You don't know nothing about this trap music, do you? You know about the rapper Gucci?"

Terrell said. "I never heard of him before," I said. Terrell asked if we wanted to smoke or drink and I quickly said, "no" while, Toya said, "yes!" She said it in a hysteric way and began to drink and smoke with them. As the night went on, they continued to get high and drunk and I was the only sober one. I really didn't feel comfortable.

I really wanted to leave, but I just couldn't leave Toya. I guess I could stay a little longer, so she can sober up, before we go back in the house. Next thing you know Toya began to say, "Shay you need to let Terrell take your virginity. Why are you still a virgin girl? Let him feel on those big breasts, that's what God gave you them for. They are to let a man feel on you." They all began to laugh while, Terrell and Cory started giving Toya praise saying, "We like this girl and we have to keep her around." They all thought it was funny, but I felt humiliated. I didn't even know him like that, but she was so drunk she didn't even know what she was saying. Out of nowhere my cousin, Toya, goes upstairs with Cory and leaves me downstairs with Terrell. I don't know what to do at this point. Why would my cousin leave me alone with this man I barely know? At this point, I am so frightened, I just want to go home. But, I can't leave my cousin and I don't know how to get out of this house with all the wood blocking the doors. I guess, I'm just going to have to play it cool.

Terrell and I began to talk for a second, then out of nowhere he looked me straight in my face, his eyes were blood shot red, he really looked out of it, and he says, "Take your pants off." My heart sank to my stomach and I became silent, as I thought to myself what do I do? My cousin is upstairs drunk and she is not in her right mind and there's no way out of this house. I think that Terrell is so under the influence that he is not in his right mind. I'm so afraid of what he will do to me, if I say no. So, I began to take my pants off. I heard a wrapper opening and I saw that he was putting a condom on. So, I quickly said "what are you doing." He looked at me with the dirtiest look I have ever seen in my life and said harshly, "What the fuck you mean, what I'm doing." The way he spoke, the tone of his voice and his whole demeanor frightened me to the point where I was going to do anything he said, just so he would not hurt me.

After he put the condom on, he told me to lay down. I looked up at his face and knew he was not going to stop, until he gets what he wants. So, I laid down on the bed and he began to get on top of me and tried to force himself inside of me. It hurt so bad that I began to try and push him off me while saying, "Stop." But, it seemed as if he didn't hear me. He was just smiling like the pain I was feeling was pleasing him. Or, maybe he was in a blackout. I really don't know what was wrong with him, but then again I barely know him. He tried to push harder and harder to break through my vaginal walls. While he kept pushing the pain got worse and worse and the tears began to flow from my eyes, but he would not stop. I just can't believe that I am getting my virginity taken from someone that I just met. I just wish I would have never chosen to come over here and then this would never be happening.

He suddenly stopped and I rushed to the bathroom, with my clothes half way off. It was dark and dingy in there. The sink was over flown and there was just a little bit of tissue left for me. I wiped myself and I realized that I was bleeding. How can this be happening to me? I just had my virginity took from a man that I don't even know? I always thought I was going to lose my virginity to the man that I am in love with and we would be married. I pictured me losing my virginity to the man that loved me and that would have taken his time with me, but it's too late now. I felt all my self-worth, confidence and self-esteem just leave and I wasn't the same Shay anymore.

I went back into the room and just started crying harder. Terrell began to say, "What's wrong and asked if he was whack or something?" This man doesn't even realize the pain and suffering he just put me through. I don't think he believed that I was a virgin or maybe those drugs really had him in a different world. I looked at the time and I see that it was after 12:00 am I couldn't go home this late. I am so ashamed. I can't even look anyone in the face right now. I ended up falling asleep on the bed, next thing you know I woke up to a man tapping me on my butt saying, "Baby girl, go lay on the couch." I don't know this man, but this is the second time I have been violated in one night. I felt I couldn't do anything about it, but do what this older man said and go lay on the couch. I didn't know where Toya, Terrell or Cory was. This just seems like a nightmare that I am not waking up from.

Around 4:00 in the morning, I heard banging at the window and the man that kicked me out of the bedroom, went into the kitchen, stepped on a ladder and got something out of the roof and then handed it to the person out the window. I quickly realized that I was in a drug house and Terrell must be a drug dealer. I did not belong there, I'm so cold I just want to go home. All I can do was cry myself back to sleep, wishing that this was a nightmare that I will soon wake up from. That morning I woke up to the same older man hitting me on my butt saying "Get up baby girl, your friends are upstairs." I quickly ran upstairs. I see Terrell, Toya and Cory all laying in the bed together. Why would they leave me alone downstairs? This was one of the worst nights of my life. So, I woke Toya up and said, "We have to go."

I got to go home and tell my mom some reason why I didn't come home last night. But, I don't know what to tell her. I can't tell her the truth, because she would be so hurt and disappointed in me. So, Toya ended up calling our friend Donna to come get us and acted like we stayed at her house last night.

I finally got home, walked in the house and my mom instantly started crying when she saw me. She screamed, "Where have you been? I been worried about you all night." I told her I was at Donna's house, but I know she didn't believe me. This was the first time I ever lied to my mom and it didn't feel good. She continued to cry and said don't ever do anything like that again. It hurt me so bad to see my mom hurt, but she doesn't even know how I'm am hurting on the inside right now.

I went upstairs to my room and just thought about everything that happened last night. What am I going to do next? I don't want to ever talk to Terrell again, but he did just take my virginity. I don't know what to do at this point. I can't tell anyone what really happened to me. I'm just ashamed. What if he tells someone he had sex with me? Maybe I should lie and act like the sex was mutual and I wanted him to take my virginity. I was always taught that you must wait until marriage and you should only have sex with one person. Maybe I have to stay with Terrell now that he took my virginity. I honestly don't know what to do and I wouldn't want anyone to ever find out what really happened. There are so many thoughts running through my mind. I just don't know what I should do.

Chapter Two

Life - Changing Decision

It's been almost a year now and I just graduated High School! Walking across that stage is one of the best feelings in the world. I went and got my license and my mom bought me a nice little car for graduating, 1998 Gold Saturn. I also settled a job at a nursing home, so I am doing well for myself right now.
However, I party a lot more now. I like going out and having fun, riding around, smoking weed and drinking alcohol! I love chilling with my home girls, going to concerts and just enjoying myself. This is the most fun I had in my life!

If you're wondering if I continued to talk to Terrell after that night? The answer is yes. Why? Honestly, I don't even know why. I lied and told people that we were together and I finally lost my virginity to my boyfriend. I acted like that night never happened and I never let anyone know the truth not even Toya. I just would never want anyone to find out what really happened to me, because it's his word against mines. I am too ashamed. I don't know why I continued to deal with him after that night, it may have been because I felt obligated to stay with him, because he took my virginity or maybe I felt all my self-worth leave that night. I prided myself on being a virgin and waiting until I get married to have sex. Yes, I came close a couple times, but the person knew how to stop when I said "stop." My whole innocence left me that night and I guess I thought I had no other choice then to make it work with the one who took my virginity from me. I guess, I buried what happened that night deep down inside and acted as if it never took place. All I do is get high and drunk every night. I'm just not the same person anymore.

Terrell and I have still been having sex, but it's mutual now. We really didn't use a condom the last time. So, I just went to the doctors to get on some type of birth control, because Terrell keeps saying, "I'm about to get pregnant."

I don't know what I would do if that happened! I have to wait for my menstrual to come, then I can start taking my birth control pills and I won't have any worries.

It's been a couple weeks now, and I know that my menstrual should have been on, so that I can take these pills. I should make sure that I am not pregnant. So, my home girl, Nae Nae, and I went to the local store to pick up a pregnancy test. Terrell and I would use protection most of the time, but sometimes we didn't. I should take this test just to make sure that I am not pregnant.

When we got back to my house, we head straight to the bathroom. I looked at the pregnancy test box and followed all the instructions. I waited two minutes like the direction said, before I read the result. My mind was everywhere. My stomach was getting butterflies, as I was patiently waiting for the results that can possibly change my life forever.

Finally, the two minutes passed and I took a deep breath, before I read the result. I slowly picked up the stick and I see two bright blue lines. My heart just starts to beat faster and faster as my palms began to get sweaty. I looked at the box to read the direction again and it clearly says, two lines means you're pregnant. No, this can't be happening to me right now, not me. I can't have a child right now. I'm only eighteen and I'm still a child myself.

I quickly snapped back into reality, when my home girl Nae Nae said, "What does it say?" With tears rolling down my face all I could do was look at her and say, "I'm pregnant." Finally, I pulled myself together and went downstairs to let my mom know what is going on.

I really don't know how she is going to take it, but I hope she does not get upset with me, I need her more now than I ever did before. I went to my mom and told her I have something I must show her. I didn't know how to tell her, especially since she still thinks I'm a virgin. So, I showed her the test and all she did was smile and say, "You're not pregnant, you haven't done anything." I said, "Its real mom." Surprisingly she was happy and said, "We have to set you up a doctor's appointment."

Okay, I am somewhat relieved, because I told my mother, but now I must tell Terrell. I went by his house and picked him up and parked my car in my drive way at home. I had a serious look on my face, because I didn't know how he was going to react. When he got in the car, I pulled the pregnancy test out of my purse and handed it to him and said, "I'm pregnant." He kind of looked shocked. He had a smirk on his face and all he said was, "Okay, what are you going to do?" "I guess I'm going to keep it", I said, and he said, "Alright!"

I was able to get an appointment to see a doctor and its official. I am five weeks pregnant and my due date is March 24, 2009. The doctors found out I was still smoking weed, when they gave me a drug test, but I'm going to quit now. Honestly, I just want to have fun with my friends, but I can't anymore because I'm pregnant. At least Terrell and I have been spending more time together. He said that, "he wants us to move in together." But, I don't think that is a good idea. I know I am having his child, but honestly, I am not about to move with a man and leave my family.

I don't know the first thing about taking care of a baby. Terrell isn't a family man. He is the type of dude that likes to be out all night getting money and I will not be left in the house all day with the baby by myself. I just lost my job at the nursing home, because I called in too many times, I wasn't feeling good because of this pregnancy. I can't depend on him to take care of me.

I guess me getting pregnant and moving into an apartment together was Terrell's plans, because ever since I said no he started telling me to get an abortion. He doesn't want a baby right now. I'm already four months now and I am not about to get an abortion. What is he thinking? How can he switch up like that? Now, he is ignoring my calls and when he does answer, he says stop calling him and hangs up! Is he really doing all of this, because I don't want to play house with him? We are not married and I don't have to live with him.

I haven't seen or talked to Terrell in about a month, so I called him and said, "Why have you been treating me so mean?" Then he just started being rude for no reason, he said, "I never wanted to have a baby with you. I wanted to have a baby with somebody that looked like a model, a light skinned girl or someone who was Dominican. I want her to be tall with long hair. I don't want to have a baby by you. Now stop calling my phone bitch, click!" Wow, did he really say that and hang up on me. He just described everything that I am not. I'm dark skinned, short and I have short hair. If I had any self-esteem before, he just took it all from me.

Tears rushed down my face, as I laid in my bed. All I can do was cry. I really wish I was not pregnant with his child. I don't want to have this baby anymore. As these evil thoughts came to my head, I began to squeeze my stomach with my hands hoping that I would lose this baby that the father doesn't want. I cried harder and harder, as I tried to hurt the baby that was growing inside of me. Finally, I stopped, this isn't the way to do this I must be strong and I'm going to get through this. I just wish I can talk to someone, anyone that knew what I was feeling. I just kept trying to reach out to Terrell, but he continued to reject me. I can't let anyone know how he is treating me, I don't want everyone to hate him. I just don't know what to do.

Today is the day I go to find out what I am having, my mom is with me. But, of course, Terrell wouldn't come. I am so excited. The ultrasound technician says the baby is looking healthy and the gender is a baby girl! Yes, I wanted a little girl! I guess you can say I am little happier about this whole pregnancy, because it is a baby girl. I called Terrell, he answered and I let him know it was a girl and he said, "I don't want no girl, I want a son." Here he goes again, trying to bring me down, I just don't understand what is wrong with him.

I'm about six months pregnant now and my home girl, Nae Nae, comes and tell me that Terrell was seen at a local restaurant with some girl. My heart just sunk to my stomach! While I'm sitting in the house starving, wishing I can go out to eat, he is taking the next woman to dinner. What about the woman that is carrying your child? I live with my parents and seven other brothers and sisters, so there isn't always food in the house to eat. I'm not working anymore, so I can't just go and get something to eat if I wanted to.

There have been times when we didn't have enough food and I couldn't eat, but one meal a day. But Terrell never cares, he would never check and make sure I ate. He rather chase after another female and feed her. It hurts so bad to be treated like you don't exist. I just never thought I would be in this place.

 I'm about eight months now. I had to sell my car, because I had no money at all. It just seems like everything I had was slowly taken away from me. I have no job; no car and I am about to have a baby! I never thought I would be in the place I am in right now. And to make matters worse, I received a call from an unknown number and you wouldn't believe who it was calling me from jail, Terrell! I guess he got caught with some drugs and now he is about to go away for maybe a year. Now he is trying to tell me he loves me and he is sorry for the way he has been acting. I was happy when he said all of that and I thought he was sincere, so I believed him.

 Around my due date, Terrell's lawyer said that he can get him out of jail to be at the baby's birth. I guess I'm happy, but he missed out on so much more. He wouldn't come to any doctor appointment, ultrasound appointments and he missed our baby shower. I just wish he was there for me through this whole process. All I have is my mom. If she wasn't there with me, I don't know what I would do.

Chapter Three

My First Love

It's almost midnight and I can't sleep, so I guess I'll relax, take a hot bath and listen to some gospel music. It should help ease my mind. Out of nowhere, I feel a sharp cramp in my lower stomach. I didn't think much of it, until I felt another one about ten minutes later. I hurried up and washed up, dried off and put my clothes on. It was about one o'clock in the morning by now. I kept getting these cramps and they started coming a little closer now. So, I went downstairs and woke my mom up and said, "Mom I think I'm about to have the baby." She says, "No you're not. You can't be." I don't know why she doesn't believe me. My due date is tomorrow. I sat there a little longer, but I couldn't handle the pain anymore. A sharp cramp came and all I can do was scream and say, "Mommy call the ambulance, I'm about to have the baby!"

  The ambulance finally came and the pain is beginning to become unbearable. Their asking me questions and I can't answer them until the pain goes away. I finally could tell them all the info and now my mom and I are on our way to the hospital. We pulled up to Hyland Hospital and they came out with a wheel chair for me. They rushed me to the intake room and made me change into a gown. The doctor checked my cervix and she said you are six centimeters dilated and we must get you into a room. I can barely hold a conversation with her, because this pain is so intense. My mom is laughing and saying, "Those pains aren't no joke." "Mom this is not the time to crack jokes. It hurts so bad," I said.

I made it to my room and they asked me if I want to get an epidural to help with the pain? I answered quickly, "Yes I do." This pain is turning me into a different person. I am hollering at my mother for no reason. I can't wait for this to be over. The pain subsided, as the epidermal started kicking in and look who comes walking through the door, Terrell and his mom. I guess my mom called them and let them know I was in labor. A couple hours later my aunt Julia and my cousin Sharon walked through the door. I'm real close to pushing this baby out and all I can think about is this pregnancy being over with. I can't wait to get back to myself, no more crying, no more stressing, just me going back to having fun.

The doctor came in and checked my cervix and said, "Your 10 centimeters' now, you can push!" All I can do is smile. 9 hours of labor and I can finally start pushing. My family came over and helped me hold my legs up, so that I can start pushing, while Terrell just stood in the corner and looked through magazines. Yea, I am kind of upset, because he didn't really talk to me this whole time or try to comfort me through this pain, but it's almost over. I began to push. When the Doctor said push, I couldn't really feel myself pushing, because the epidural numbed my lower body. So, I tried pushing again and I suddenly began to feel my baby girl slowly coming out. As I heard a cry, I knew my baby girl was delivered safely.

The doctor's put her on my chest and I just looked in her eyes with adoration. I already loved my baby girl. It's time now to cut the umbilical cord and even though Terrell wouldn't look while I was giving birth, he came over to cut the cord! The doctors quickly put her on the scale. She weighs 6 pounds 11 ounces and she is 18 ½ inches. I'm really amazed at this moment. I can't believe I have a child now. I'll name her Ayanna Diane Burgess.

While everyone left to go home, Terrell decided to stay the night with me at the hospital. I was kind of shocked, but thankful at the same time. I didn't really want to be there alone. He went over to the baby and was just watching her. Then out of nowhere he says, "Why are her ears so dark she better not be dark skinned." Is he serious, even if our daughter turns out dark skinned, she will still be beautiful. Why would he even say that? I couldn't even respond back to him. I'm just about to go to sleep. I'm tired and I had a long day.

It's time to go home with the baby. I enjoyed my stay at the hospital. They were so helpful and they blessed me with so many packs of diapers and milk. I'm still in pain, but the first thing I did was look in the mirror. I can't believe the way my body changed. I have so many stretch marks and my stomach is still big. Before I had the baby, I use to love wearing half shirts and showing off my stomach, but I guess those days are over with. I'm kind of feeling a little depressed, this is not what I'm used to. I never thought my body would look like this.

Chapter Four

Reality Set In

It's been about a month and Terrell had to go back to jail to finish his sentence. He has about a year. My daughter is doing great. I have been looking for a job, so that I can provide for my daughter. But, it seems like no one will hire me. Having a child is a lot harder than I thought it would be. My whole life must revolve around her now. She constantly needs diapers, wipes, milks, bigger clothes and it's so hard, when you don't have the money to take care of your baby needs. My mom helps me whenever she can, but she has her own children she must take care of.

My daughter is getting bigger so fast and she can't fit into anything. I really need a job. I have been putting so many applications in on the internet and I still can't get a job, I don't know what to do. I wish her father was not in jail, so that he can help me.

My mom saw I needed things for the baby, so she ended up calling this non-profit organization to get me an appointment to go get used clothes for my daughter. Anything would help me right now. I went to the appointment with my mom and got my daughter plenty of clothes, socks and little toys. They also gave one pack of diapers. Honestly, before I had my daughter I would be embarrassed to be getting hand me downs, but I must provide for my baby, by any means necessary.

I have some clothes for her now, but she doesn't have any milk or wipes and I don't have a dollar to my name. My mom hasn't had any money lately since the Feds bust in our house and took most of our resources. I really don't know what to do. Nae Nae and I walked to the corner store and I saw they were selling a little can of formula for 2 dollars. I really don't have 2 dollars to buy my daughter some milk. I'm not use to struggling like this. I looked at Nae Nae and asked her if she had 2 dollars and she said yea! It took a lot of pride out of me to ask her for money. I've never had to ask anyone for anything, especially 2 dollars, but I will do anything for my daughter. I guess I can just use a wash cloth for my daughter, until I get the other 2 dollars for some wipes.

Being a parent is so hard, Ayanna is about 5 months now and I still haven't found a job. I'm so stressed and angry that I am taking care of this baby alone. Every time I think about her father being in prison and me having to take on the full responsibility of raising this child, I get so angry inside. It's just not fair. I never thought I would be 19 years old raising a baby alone, struggling to come up with money to buy her anything. I just wish I had a way of an escape. I can't even hang with my friends anymore. I'm not the same person and it hurts, when I realize how my life has changed so drastically.

With all these pressures of life weighing me down, I decided to go to church with my mom. I really needed God to move on my behalf, because I don't know how much more I can take of this. The word was good, but it just wasn't enough. But one lady, I didn't catch her name, a Caucasian woman, petite, with short blond hair, just happened to come to me and ask me what do I need God to do for me? Tears began to flow from my eyes, "I really need a job." As I spoke those words, I honestly felt that God was hearing me. I can't explain it, but I know that he heard my cry! So, the lady began to pray that the Lord fulfilled my every need. While she was praying I just felt such a calmness, it just felt like all my worries were gone. Later that day I went to my Aunt Julia's house to fill out some more job applications. I'm so ready to start working, so that I can provide for my baby. The next day I was expecting a call from a job, but I didn't receive a call. That didn't discourage me, because I know the Lord won't let me down.

    I was sleeping so well and suddenly my phone rang. I answered and all I heard was a man's voice asking to speak to Shay Burgess. "This is me speaking", I said. "Hello, this is Larry calling from Target and would like to know if you would like to come in for an interview today", he said. "Yes, I can." He gave me all the information and asked me to be there in an hour. I jumped up so fast and said thank you Jesus. I can't believe I just put this application, in for this job, on Sunday right after church and they called me for an interview on Tuesday.

    I went to the interview. I had to go through three managers to get hired. The last manager came to me and said, "Can you take your drug test today?" I anxiously said, "Yes." I am really in disbelief that I got the job so fast. I will never forget what God did for me. I knew He was going to bless me and I believed and He didn't let me down.

    I have been working hard. Five days a week and 9-hour shift. I barely see my daughter, but I must do what was best for her. I'm thankful for my mom. She watches her, while I am at work. Working all day and then having to come home and take care of my daughter is difficult. I have been trying to find ways to relieve my stress, so I started going out to the club more. Once I put my daughter to sleep, I leave. Usually every Friday, my homegirls and I get drunk and go out to the club. It feels just like the old days, when I didn't have any responsibilities. I can just have fun.

When I go out to party, I feel my age. When I am home with my baby and working, I feel like I am in my 40s. I just wish I can act my age and do the things that my friends are doing. Getting drunk every weekend and living that night life has been changing me for the worse a little. But this is the only way I know how to deal with what I'm going through, by getting drunk. I guess this is the only time I can forget about all my responsibilities as a mother. Going out and getting attention from men and everyone begging to get your number feels good. Especially, when I just got dogged by the father of my child. He treats me like crap while every other man begs to be with me and they will do anything in their power to make it happen.

My mom has been telling me that I need to slow down and stop going out so much and stay at home with my daughter. Honestly, I'm not trying to hear that. I'm trying to have fun. I had been sitting in the house for nine months pregnant, depressed and stressed out. I just want to have a good time. She may be right, because I have been having bad dreams lately about going out partying all the time. I just had a dream that I was leaving the club and some random man just came up and shot me directly in my head and I died. I been having a lot of these dreams lately. Well, I'm still going to have fun and party. It was just a dream.

You know what today is, Friday! I'm just getting off work and my homeboy Bryan just hit me up and asked if my homegirls and I wanted to come by his party. I'm hype, so I hit my girls Marra, Yalonda, and Toya up and they were down. So, we decided to go. When we got there, it was a cool atmosphere. We saw a lot of people we knew from high school. It's always good seeing old friends.

We chilled inside for a minute then my home girls, Bryan and I went to go and get some air outside. My home girls were standing by the car talking, while I was talking to Bryan. I was sitting on the hood of his truck, but something told me to go talk to my home girls. So, I told Bryan, "I'll be right back." He said "alright," and walked away. So, I walked directly to the car my homegirls were by. Not even 30 seconds later all I heard was about 10 gun shots go off. People were screaming and running from different directions. We quickly got in the car and Bryan came running, in the car too. We hurried and drove off. We made sure everyone was alright and we all just took a deep breath. We are thankful that we are all safe.

We drove around for a second, but we had to go back to the party to drop Bryan off to his car. When we pulled up to his truck, all you saw was glass all over the ground. All his windows were shot up! At this moment, all I can think about is me and if I never got off his car. I would have been the one shot! I don't know why something told me to go to the other car with my girls and leave his car, but I am thankful that I did. Well, let me go home and hold my daughter. I could have been taken from her tonight.

I finally talked to Bryan and got the scoop on what happened at the party! I guess some dude got robbed, while he was in the party. He left, came back and just started shooting. Man, you never know when or where death lies. You must make sure you aren't at the wrong place at the wrong time. Anyone could have been murdered that night, because of one person lack of judgment. I'm just glad that no one got hurt.

Chapter Five

Finding The Truth

    My daughter is almost one now and I have been working so much that it seems like I have missed out on her growing up. My mom always was the one to watch her do everything first, like the first time she sat up by herself or the first time she crawled and started walking. Honestly, I don't want to miss out on my daughter's growth anymore. I think I'm about to quit my job. I rather be with my daughter. Plus, I have a good amount of money saved up to get her what she need. I didn't put my two weeks' notice in. I just stopped going. I know that was wrong, but I couldn't go to that job another day and be away from my daughter. The only time I would see her was at night and she would be sleeping.

    My baby's father just got out of jail and he is being real cool. We are getting along! He told me he needed to get back on his feet and he needed my help. I didn't know what he meant by that, so he explained more. He asked me to lend him some money, so he can buy some drugs to sell and he will give me double what I let him borrow. I don't really know what to do. Can I trust him? He is my baby's father, so I don't think he would pull a fast one on me and I did just quit my job, so I need the extra money. So, I said alright and went to the bank and withdrew $800 dollars and gave it to him. He had the biggest grin on his face and said, "I got you as soon as I get it."

It's now my daughters first birthday and I haven't really asked Terrell about the money he owed me, because he would always say he still working on it! I have been low on money, ever since I gave him that money. I asked him for money to help with our daughter's birthday party and he said he didn't have it. I don't understand how he doesn't have money, when I just gave him $800 not even a month ago, So, I had to go to the mall and take back the $120 sneakers that he bought me for my birthday that I never wore! Then, I went to the store and bought my daughter everything she needed for her birthday party and it was a success. She enjoyed herself.

Terrell has been acting real shady lately, ever since I gave him that money. Every time I would call him and ask him about my money, he gets upset. I don't know what's going on, but my daughter needs things and I need some money. So, one day I just end up calling him, because I really didn't have any money for my daughter's diapers. I asked him, "Do you have my money?" and he literally said, "Stop calling my phone bitch, I'm not giving you shit," and hung up the phone on me. My eyes started to burn, as tears started to build up. How can he do this to us? I looked out for him, because he just got out of jail and I let him borrow money. He was just going to treat me like crap. I wish I never gave him anything.

I'm stressed out again and I just wish my problems would go away. Something's got to give. My home girl Donna and my cousin Toya have been trying to get me to come to this church they have been going to. I might go, because I need some peace. They said this church really helped them and they stopped smoking weed and drinking, ever since they started going there. One thing I know is that if church can stop them two from smoking weed, which they smoked like 10 blunts a day, I know it's real. I used to be with them smoking every day and they never stopped.

I decided to go to church with them. I will never forget. It was Wednesday, March 31, 2010. I remember walking through the church doors. It was a small church. They had the lights dim and there were only a few people in the building. The preacher began to preach and I instantly felt that he was preaching to me and my exact situation I am in. He started to talk about God and how He will provide for you and your children and you don't have to keep begging your baby father to do anything. I didn't even have my daughter with me but I knew he was speaking to me. He started saying to forgive that person who owes you money. How does this pastor know exactly what I am going through? For him just saying that God can help you through it all, it just gave me so much peace. That day I gave my life to the Lord, because I know that having the Lord on my side is the only way I can deal with what I am going through.

I continued to go the church, Love and Worship. I began to learn a lot about Jesus Christ. I have always known God and I would pray to Him every day and read my bible since I was a little girl, but there is so much to Him that I didn't know, until now. Pastor Washington, began to preach about the club. Christians don't belong in the club and asked what does darkness have in common with light and I listened. I still go out, but no one ever told me that it was wrong to do so. So, after church I asked the pastor does he really think that Christians shouldn't go to the club. He said "We are supposed to be set apart and living a life of holiness. If you are in the club with the sinners how are you different from them." I understood what he was saying, but I still went out that same night. Honestly, when I walked into the club I didn't feel the same way as I used to feel. I use to go out to meet men and get drunk and dance all on somebody. I couldn't even enjoy myself, especially since I was sober, I just want to go back to church and feel that peace again.

I have been still trying to work things out with Terrell and trying to have him give me my money back. It's like he just purposely tries to hurt me and make me miserable. Going to church and seeking God more is giving me more peace about this whole situation. I know me and my daughter is going to be alright!

It is now Mother's Day and I am on my way to church. I get there and there is a guest speaker from Buffalo N.Y. I didn't catch his name, but he was preaching well. At the end of his message, he told all the mothers to come up to the altar. I was hesitant, because I didn't want everyone to know I have a child and I am so young. But, I finally went up and took my daughter with me. He began to speak to each woman individually. While he spoke to them, most began to cry because of the things he was saying. When he came to speak to me, I didn't really know what to expect.

He began to tell me that I am a very happy person and I have lots of joy, but there is a stronghold! He looked me in the eyes and said, "LET HIM GO." I began to cry and I just felt a release in my heart. The preacher is right, ever since I have been coming to church and living for God, not getting drunk clubbing anymore, or having sex, I have been so happy. However, every time I end up talking to Terrell, he can easily bring me back to a place of depression and I am really going to leave him alone now. It had to be God speaking through that man, because he doesn't know me. But, that is something I am struggling with.

    I have been going to every church service and I have been reading my Bible, listening to my gospel music and praying. I have changed so much from going to this church and I have learned so much about God. I now know that you must live a holy life, to enter heaven. I've learned that you can be saved, but you must get delivered from the sin and the bad habits in your life. So, that is what I am going to do. I will not let anyone stop me from living for God. I had to stop hanging with my friends because being around them makes me want to go back to my old way of living. If they start talking about getting a bottle of liquor and going out or going to chill with dudes, I sometimes want to do those things, because I am not that strong in the Lord yet. Even living in my mother's house with all my brothers and sisters can be distracting, so I just stay in my room and seek the Lord.

Chapter Six

A Broken Promise

I still haven't talked to Terrell. He usually pops up at my house and tries to talk to me, but I just walk away and tell him to go talk to his daughter. With him out of my life, I am so much happier. He can no longer control my emotions, when he feels like it and I feel good. If he thinks we will ever be cool after he took my money and never gave me a dime back, he must be crazy. I don't have anything to say to him and I really don't want to even see his face.

Once again, I just got a call from Terrell, he is locked up and he will be doing another year. I can honestly care less at this moment. He never helped me with his daughter anyways. He wouldn't buy any diapers, wipes, clothes, formula, or anything. He wouldn't even watch her. When I asked, he would tell me he isn't watching a baby, like she isn't his child. So, if he thinks I care that he is in jail, I don't.

Church is tonight and I can't wait to get there to praise the Lord. Pastor Washington is preaching on point and the Holy Spirit is all in this church. Out of nowhere, the pastor started preaching about tongue rings and what they represent. I was really in tune with what he was saying, because I have a tongue ring in right now. I've had mostly every piercing before, my eye brow, nose, lip, tongue, belly button and 5 piercings on each ear. He began to tell us what the tongue ring represents and how it is a sign that you enjoy giving oral sex.

That is not the reason I have this piercing. But, I understood where he was coming from. That is what people assume and I don't want to be judged, because of it. As he continued to preach, I just felt the Lord tugging at my heart and telling me to take my tongue ring out and throw it on the altar. Honestly, I didn't want anyone to know I had a tongue ring, after what he said it represents. I hesitated at first, but I heard the Lord speak again, so I quickly unscrewed my tongue piercing, walked up in front of the church and threw it on the alter. I immediately started to cry, I felt a release in my body. I just knew that God was pleased with my obedience.

Soon after I went back to my seat Pastor Washington called me back up and said, "God is pleased with you." He let everyone know what I just did and said that from me being obedient God is going to bless me. He asked me what I needed God to do for me. I told him I needed an apartment, a car and a job. He laid his hands on my forehead and prayed that the Lord blesses me with everything I need. Then out of nowhere, a couple stood up and said that, "The Holy Spirit told them to bless me with their car." They just bought a new car and they were going to sell their old car, but God told them to bless me with it. I immediately began to cry and praise the Lord for putting me on their heart and having them be sympathetic to my needs.

Later after church, the wife gave me all their information and told me to call them in the morning. Of course, I called the next day. I looked at the card for their name and asked for Mrs.

Rodan. I told her that I was the young lady from church last night and she began to sound ecstatic. She went on and on about how she used to be a single mother, before she met her husband and she knows the struggle.

She also let me know that the car was a 1998 Camry and she was so happy, when the Lord put it on her spirit to give the car to me. We talked a little while longer then she told me to call her later, so we can figure out a date for me to come pick the car up.

I haven't talk to Terrell and he has not given me any money, so I need a job. Any job will be good right now. I just don't want to work all day and be away from my daughter. So, my sister, Michelle, and I end up going to Wendy's and putting an application in, then we asked to speak to the manager. When we spoke to the manager he told us both to come in tomorrow for an interview. We went to the interview and we both got the job! Now, I am about to go over to Sycamore Green apartments and put an application in, so that me and my daughter can move out of my mom's house. The rent is 30% of your income so that is good.

I can't believe that God is answering my prayers so quickly. Turning my life over to Him has been one of the best decision that I could have made, in my life. I'm just so glad that I listened to the Lord, when He told me to take that tongue ring out and throw it on the altar. Whatever God wants me to do, I will do it. He has shown me a new, better way of living and I am so honored that He choose me to live for Him.

I have been calling the Rodan's for about a week now and they haven't answered or returned any of my calls. They haven't even been to church, since that night. I don't know what's going on, but I have to see about the car they promised me. I went around and talked to some of the other church members and they began to tell me that the Rodan's weren't coming back to this church anymore.

    Wait, hold on, they were just members of this church. They were actually leaders in this church and now when they tell me that they are going to bless me with a car, they no longer attend this church. I guess that's the reason they haven't been returning any of my calls. They aren't going to give me the car, as they promised me. They probably aren't coming back to the church, because they publicly announced it in front of the whole church that they were going to give me their car and they can't tell the truth and own up to their lie.

    What the Rodan's did could have broken me and caused me not to trust people in the church. It could have stopped me from coming to church all together. I could have gotten discouraged and my faith could have been shaken. But, I know that regardless of what people do, God, himself, will never hurt me or want to purposely humiliate me. They may have made a promise that they could not keep, but God will always keep His promises to me. I'm just thankful that I have such a great relationship with the Lord, that I will not let anything or anyone take me away from God's love.

Chapter Seven

New Beginnings

I just received the call that I am number 3 on the waiting list, for the apartment I applied for. I am so excited. I'm going in today for my interview, they will let me know when I can start moving in! I can't believe that my daughter and I are going to be on our own soon. It is going to be so peaceful, at my house. No loud music, no one screaming at the top of their lungs, no arguing, just me and my daughter. Of course, I am going to miss living with my family. I love them, but I have to be in a place where I can seek God and hear His voice, when He is trying to speak to me.

It's the first of the month and I just got the keys to my apartment. I don't really have anything to bring besides our clothes, but I'm still thankful. I didn't really think about furniture, when I decided I wanted to move. Even if I did think about it, I still didn't have the funds to buy furniture anyways. I will make the best out of what I have. Everything is falling into place. I have a job, an apartment and all I need now is my car.

I'm having a hard time transitioning from my mother's house to my new apartment, especially since me and my daughter have to sleep on the floor at our place. There's no television, no internet, just a radio that I can play my gospel music on. It's also difficult because now I must take my daughter on the bus, before I go to work and drop her off at my mother's house. Before, I could leave, go to work and come back, but now it's so much more than what I am accustomed to. I still stay at my mother's house from time to time, but it's time for me to be consistent with staying home so that I can get used to it.

I just started my college courses and I also picked up another job, as lunch-aid in a school that I used to attend when I was younger. I'm a little burnt out having to get up so early and travel on the bus to do everything. To make matters worse, the bus stop is about a mile from my home. I just wish that the Rodan's would have really blessed me with that car because I really need it right now. It's so hard getting around on the bus, I do everything on the bus. I have to drop my daughter off to my mother, then catch the next bus to make it to my job at the school, quickly after that I have to catch the bus to get to my classes and then when my classes are over I have to take the bus to make it to my job at Wendy's. Then, around 11 at night, head to my mother's house to pick up my daughter and then get right back on the bus again to get back home. Lord, please bless me with a car. I don't know how much longer I can do this, especially in this weather. It was really 6 below 0 and it hurts me to see my daughter freezing while we get around on the bus.

Beep, beep, beep, my alarm has been going off all morning and I finally got the strength to get up and check the time. Oh, my Gosh, I over slept and the bus comes in 15 minutes. I hurried up and threw some clothes on, brushed my teeth, washed my face, got my daughter dressed and rushed out the door. It is freezing outside and my daughter won't stop crying, she is so tired and this cover isn't keeping her warm at all in this negative degree weather.

Journey of a Single Mother

When I thought, it couldn't get any worse, I just saw the bus ride by and the next one isn't coming for another half an hour.

Stop crying princess mommy got you, everything is going to be alright, God is going to bless us. I swear, I wouldn't wish this struggle on my worst enemy. Honestly, I can handle this weather and constant traveling but my daughter doesn't deserve to go through this, no child does. I'm so broken hearted, because my child must suffer and go through with me. I just wish I had a car. Lord Jesus, please bless me and my daughter with transportation. Out of nowhere, this car pulls up at the bus stop and asks me if we need a ride somewhere. When I looked in the car, it was a Caucasian lady. I was skeptical about getting in at first, because I didn't know her, but my daughter was too cold not to take this ride. I quickly said yes, opened the door of the front seat and held my daughter on my lap. "Thank you so much," I said, with gratitude, she doesn't even know that she was like an angel to me. She said, "You're welcome no one deserves to be walking outside in this weather, especially someone with a baby." I told her where I needed to go and she took me. I know that her picking us up was God's way of telling me that He is here with me and He hears my cries. Thank you, Jesus.

Chapter Eight

God Heard My Cries

It's been about a year and I still don't have a car and I never heard anything from the Rodan's. I'm so discouraged right now, because God said that He was going to bless me with a car. I didn't think I would have to struggle this long and it's making my faith get weary. I will always believe in You God, but right now my circumstances are causing me to doubt You. I have been trying my hardest to live holy. I attend every church service and I also sing on the praise team and sing solos, whenever I am asked. Why aren't You blessing me God? Why am I struggling so much? I really thought, when I decided to live for You, that life wouldn't be so hard. Lord, I need answers! I prayed and prayed to my Lord and I heard Him say, "I will never leave you or forsake you, daughter, I will bless you when the time is right." Just hearing God's voice began to calm me down. All I needed was to hear Him say those words and my faith stayed strong.

Now, it's time to pray about this car situation. Lord, how am I going to get a car, when I don't have the funds to buy one? I stopped talking and tried to hear his voice, suddenly I heard him say, call Spesh and ask him to help you buy a car. Spesh is my first cousin. He is one of the best well known rappers in the town, but he just gave me money a few months ago, to help me buy some stuff for my apartment. I was able to get me a nice full size blow up bed, TV, and a DVD player, some things for my daughter and I paid a couple bills. He has done enough for me, but if You are telling me to ask him God I will do it. I may feel uncomfortable but I know that there is a reason you are telling me to call him.

I don't have his number, so I called my mom to get it, I know she has his number. I took a deep breath, before I called and gathered my thoughts. I slowly dialed the number, and as the phone began to ring my heart began to race faster. "Who is this?" Spesh said. "This is Shay," I replied. "What up little cuz?" "Um, I have to ask you a question but I'm afraid to ask." He said, "Go ahead." I quickly said, "Can you please give me some money, so that I can buy me a car, it's just so hard taking my daughter around on the bus, can you help me?" He was quiet, then he asked how much I needed, I told him $5,000. He began to laugh while saying, "That's a lot of money, I don't have it right now, let me see what I can do." "Okay, thank you," I replied, and we got off the phone. I don't know if he is really going to help me, especially since he laughed at how much I asked for, but at least I faced my fears and was obedient to God and called.

It's been a few months and I haven't heard back from my cousin, Spesh. I just happened to be getting off the bus with my daughter and was walking to my mother's house and he was there. I didn't have the courage to go up to him and ask him about the money, because at the end of the day he doesn't owe me anything and he doesn't have to give me anything. I just waved at him and walked into my mom's house. As much as I need a car, I just must patiently wait for God to bless me. I know He will.

I'm on my way to church tonight and I am ready to go and give God some praise. I got in the building and I immediately felt God's presence. I just began to thank Him in the corner of the church, I began to think about all the times I would cry at night because of how my baby's father would treat me. I also began to think about all the times I didn't have any money and I couldn't afford to buy my daughter anything, not even a pack of $2 wipes. I also thought about the nights that I was out partying, just wanting a man to pay attention to me, because I lacked self-esteem. I relived the night, when I could have been shot to death, if I didn't listen to that voice telling me to move. I remembered the night when I was debating if I should give my daughter up for adoption because I felt I couldn't handle raising her alone. The stress and depression I felt raising her alone. I thought back to the nights when I would ask the Lord to take my life because I did not want to live anymore. If I died at least I know my daughter would have been well taken care of by my mother.

As I thought of all these things that happened in my past, I just began to lift my hands with tears flowing consistently down my face and say, "Thank you, Jesus!" Thank you, Lord for protecting me. I could have been dead, but you spared my life. I could have committed suicide, all because of deep depression. But, Lord, you kept my mind through everything and I am so thankful I have peace now. I don't care if you don't allow me to get a car or answer any prayers that I have prayed, God I'm just thankful that you brought me out of everything I have been through.

I was the only one in the church that seemed to feel the Holy Ghost screaming, "Hallelujah, thank you, Jesus," but I didn't care what anyone thought about me. They don't know what God has done for me and the things that He has brought me out of. He deserves my praise and much more, all I can say is, thank you, Lord.

It felt so good praising God at church last night, now I'm on my way to my mother's house just so I can see my family. I get to my mom's house and I haven't been there for more than 5 minutes and the doorbell rings. So, I get up and answer the door and it's Spesh. He comes through the door and throws some keys to me. I look at the keys in confusion, as I looked back at him. He says "Go see your car!"

I quickly ran outside to my mom's driveway and I see an all-black on black car. This car is so clean. It has the all black leather seats, sun roof, 2001 two door Honda Accord Coupe and it even has a booming system with the biggest speakers I've ever seen in the trunk. This can't be my car, this is exactly the kind of car I was asking God to bless me with. I always wanted an all-black car with a sunroof. I went back over to my cousin, he says, "You like it?" I said, "Yes, is this mine?" He said, "Yeah, I had to hurry up and get you something, since I saw you and your daughter walking that day. It really touched me and I know you were telling the truth and you needed a car." All I could do was hug him and start hysterically crying on his shoulder saying, "Thank you so much, thank you so much." "You're welcome, I do what I can," he said.

I was able to drive my car home with me that night. He had the plates on it and everything, so that I can have some time to get my car registered and insured in my name. Spesh doesn't even know how he affected my life. He literally just turned my life around today. This was the greatest blessing he could have ever done for me. He really allowed God to use him in my life and help me when no one else would. While so many people lied, and said that they would give me a car, he was the one that did it. Now, I know why I had to pray to the Lord and ask him how I was going to get a car. I am so thankful that I put my pride aside and was obedient to the Lord's voice. All I want to do right now is pray and thank the Lord for all he has done for me.

Lord, I pray that you bless my cousin Spesh, protect him everywhere he goes God, cover him in your blood and hear his inward cries. Whatever it is that he is asking You to do, I pray right now that You will manifest Yourself to him. Lord, he blessed your servant and he saw me in need. He did not shut up his bowels of compassion, so I'm asking You, Lord, to supply his every need, according to Your riches and glory. I prayed and cried and prayed some more, I just can't believe I have my car. Thank you, Jesus!

I love my new car! It drives so smooth and my daughter is so much happier now. It is so much easier now, no more walking with my daughter in below zero weather to wait on the bus. I can get to school and work on time now. I just can't believe God moved so fast for me. I was really at church last night praising and telling God that it didn't matter if He didn't allow me to get a car, I will still love him. And then the next day, my cousin just hands me the keys to a beautiful car. Lord, you are a provider and I see firsthand now.

Terrell just got out of jail and he is a changed man. He has a job now and me and him have been really getting along. He helps buy things for our daughter and we often spend time together taking her places, he even comes to church. It really feels good to have his help, this is all I wanted.

Journey of a Single Mother

    Me and Terrell ended up taking our daughter to the movies. We were in the car leaving and out of nowhere our daughter says, "daddy you are about to get shot." Me and Terrell looked at her in shock and wondered why she said that, she doesn't even know why. I was just about to drop him off but I ended up telling him to just stay the night with us tonight to make sure he is safe.

    Well, Terrell is safe so he ended up leaving in the morning while I'm on my way to church. I really can't believe Terrell didn't even try to have sex with me last night. We kissed and he didn't even try to go any further. I know he is a changed man and he respects my decision to wait because I am saved now. I really can't believe it. Well, I get to church and my pastor immediately called me up and spoke these words, "God said he is about to take someone out of your life that is causing you not to live saved." I can't believe my pastor is saying this, is that why my daughter said Terrell is going to get shot. I don't understand, how can it be Terrell and he hasn't even tried anything with me. I'm so worried now.

    Today I am going to get my car inspected and I am still thinking about what my pastor said yesterday. Out of nowhere my phone begins to ring and I see that it is Terrell's mother. Oh, Lord I hope it is not what I am thinking. I answer the phone instantly and his mother tells me that Terrell just got arrested because the Feds bust in his house and they found drugs and a gun on him. With tears in my eyes I quickly got into my car and met up with his mother.

    Terrell's mother was very emotional and she really wouldn't tell me much more. I'm really confused because I really thought Terrell stopped selling drugs and was still working, but I guess he never changed. His mom began to tell me that we must look at what happened as a blessing because just last night she had a dream that Terrell had got shot and was dead laying on the ground. Maybe God is protecting him from getting killed out here in the streets. I understood what she was saying because our daughter said the same thing, and just yesterday my pastor told me he would be gone out of my life. I'm just thankful he is safe but it really hurts to have him leave us again. I know he will be going away for a long time and my daughter needs him. I finally felt like I had help with her and life was getting easier. Why did he have to do this again? Why couldn't he just do right, now me and his daughter have to suffer from his consequences. Once again, I must raise my daughter alone I just pray that the Lord will give me the strength.

Chapter Nine

All I feel Is Fear

A few months ago, I received an application in the mail for some new housing program. I didn't really know what it was, but I filled it out and turned it in. I just went to get my mail and it was a letter from them, stating they have some newly built homes and I can come and look at the house and see if this is something I would want. They had the address on the paper, so I drove over to where the house was. Wow, it is a brand-new side by side house. I love it and I am going to move here. I quickly called the landlord and said, "I will take this house." She told me to come down and sign some paper work and I can move in by the first of the month. When I went in to sign the papers, she began to say that this home is subsidized housing and that it goes by my income. She began to look over my pay stubs and she smiled and said, "Well aren't you lucky, it looks like you don't have to pay any rent and we will give you a payment of $130 a month to help you pay for utilities." I couldn't believe what was coming out of her mouth, because I paid rent at a small apartment and now I am moving into a brand-new house, living for free and they are giving me money to help me pay my bills. This must be God. I just can't believe I am receiving all of these blessings.

Dasharra Bridges

It's the first of the month, and it's time to move in my new house. I am so excited to be starting over some place new. My mom even bought me a brand new beautiful queen sized bed, no more sleeping on a blow-up mattress. We have a real bed now. It is so beautiful in this house, there's carpet through the whole house, beautiful tile floors in the kitchen and bathroom, 2 bedrooms, 1 and ½ bathrooms, upstairs and downstairs, a big clean basement, and a big driveway. I love it here and my daughter does too.

I decided to have a sleep over at my house with my sisters and a few of my friends from church. We were having a good time doing cinnamon challenges, cracking jokes on all the people that go to church and imitating them, we were just enjoying ourselves. Then, out of nowhere, I just happen to look at the door and I see a black face and white eyes looking at me through the top window of my door. I was quickly frightened and screamed, while asking, "Did anybody else just see that man looking through the door?" No one had seen him, but me. Why would someone be looking through the windows at this time of night? It's about 3 o'clock in the morning. Who is that tall to be able to see in the top window of my door? Who is he? I know my eyes weren't playing tricks on me. I know what I had seen. This night was the beginning of the worst nightmare of my life.

I still don't know who that guy was that was looking through the window on my door. I was thinking it might have been a security guard, because I remember my landlord saying something about them having security guards to look after these houses. I decided to call and ask her. I told her there was a man that was looking through my window, "Could it have been one of your security guards?" I asked. She said, "No, the security guards are not permitted to walk on foot, they are only to look after the homes that are just built and are vacant." Now that she said that, I'm a little worried. If it wasn't a security guard, who could it be?

My cousin Ti-Ti and my home girl Lisa came to stay the night with me. We all were up late talking like we always do and suddenly we heard a knock at the door. Each of us looked up and all we saw was a black face, again, in the window of the door looking at us. When we started screaming, he ran off. I hurried up and dialed 911 to inform the police that a man is looking in my window and they said that they will send someone over. About 20 minutes later, a policeman comes to my door, out of breath, and said he caught him, he chased him for a while, but he finally caught him.

The police told me that this man was making threats to me, when they caught him. The police asked him why he was looking in my window or was he trying to steal something. Then, the man said, "I wasn't trying to steal anything. I'm a pervert." The police said, "By the way this man is talking, I need to go downtown tomorrow and go and get you an order of protection to keep you safe from this guy." The policeman gave me a police report with all the man's information on it and told me to go tomorrow and file. "Okay, officer, thank you." I looked at the paper and his name was Greg Diss. He is 54 years old and 6 feet 3 inches tall. His address was on here also, but I still don't know what he looks like.

I am so afraid now, why is this man after me? He doesn't even know me. I never been through anything like this, in my life, and I don't know how I am going to deal with this now. All I know is that, as soon as I wake up in the morning, I am going downtown and getting an order of protection against this guy.

It's been a few months and I haven't seen that man Greg looking through my windows. So, I am kind of at peace, especially after getting the order of protection. I prayed about it and I gave it to God. So, I'm not going to worry about him. Tonight, I'm having a few more of my friends come by and we are just going to cook, talk and watch a few movies. It's a little late and we all are kind of tired now. We are all in the living room and all I hear is someone breathing loudly. I don't want to say anything, because I don't know who it is, or if they just fell asleep and that's how they sound when they are asleep. I just kept watching the movie we were watching.

Suddenly, Ti-Ti began to whisper to me, "Shay, that man is looking at us through the window." My heart began to race so fast, as I began to get afraid all over again. "Call the police, call the police." As she called the police, I got up to turn the lights on and he ran off. By time the police got there, he was nowhere to be found. So, I let them know that I have an order of protection against this man and he was just at my door. They asked me if I had gotten a good look at him. I said, "I don't know what he looks like." They said, "We can't arrest anyone if you don't even know what they looked like." Basically, these cops thought it was a joke that I had an order of protection against a man whose face I haven't seen, just a reflection. They couldn't do anything and now I'm afraid for my life. If I leave my house today, I can be looking this man right in the face and not even know who he is. What do I do?

All I can do is pray now! Ask the Lord to protect me and my daughter, give me peace and help me not to live in fear. Honestly, these prayers just weren't working. I'm so scared living here and I am always coming in the house late, especially when I have church at night. We get out around 11 and then I must drop people off at home, so I get in the house around midnight, most of the time. I don't know what to do. I can't even barely sleep at night. I lock me and my daughter in the room, while we sleep at night just in case Greg Diss tries to break in. I can't live like this, why are You allowing this to happen to me, God?

I just got home from church and I can't believe I forgot to lock my doors to my car. I can't go back outside, because I am so afraid that the man is out there just waiting for me. I'm sure nothing is going to happen this one night I don't lock my door. I'm just going to go to sleep, I'm tired.

My daughter and I are getting ready to leave this morning. I must go to class and I have to drop her off at my mom's house. As we are walking outside, all I see is my doors to my car open and all my papers everywhere. I got closer to the car and I had seen that my CD players had been stolen along with the whole middle part of my dashboard. My heart just sank and all I can say is "The Lord giveth and the Lord taketh away." I can't even get mad, because this is still the car that God blessed me with and it will still get me to where I have to go. I just can't believe the one night I forget to lock my door, that's the one night it gets broken into. I really think it's Greg, the man that has been stalking me. Now, this adds another layer of fear in my life. I can't even think straight. I'm just going to miss class today and go to my mother's house and stay there for a while.

I just got home and all I can say is that it just doesn't feel the same. I really don't feel comfortable living here! If I knew it was going to be like this, I would have stayed in my old apartment, at least I felt safe living there. I wish I had a man that could protect me and my daughter, someone that will make us feel safe. But, I can't just bring anyone around my daughter. When the time is right, God will send me someone. Until then, I must be strong for my daughter. She is watching me and when I am afraid, she is frightened also. I hate seeing her cry because of this man scaring us, I just don't know what to do.

Chapter Ten

Who Can I Trust

School has been taking up a lot of my time. It is so hard to keep up with all my work, while working and attending every church service. I'm really stressed out right now. I must let something go, because I barely have time to spend with my daughter. I can't just drop out of school and I have to go to church, especially since I sing on the praise team. But, I also have to have some kind of income coming in, so that I can provide for the needs of my child. As I sat in my car before work, I began to weigh out all of my options. Suddenly, I heard a voice say, "Trust me, put your two weeks' notice in and I will provide for you." Honestly, once I heard those words, I knew it was God speaking. He has never let me down, so I know that I can trust Him. I reached in my back seat and got a piece of paper and a pen and began to write my two weeks' notice, right then. Once I walked into work, I handed it to my boss with a smile on my face, because I know that God is going to provide!

My last day of work is today and all I can say is I feel like a burden has been lifted off me. Now, I can just focus on my daughter, school and time with the Lord. Everything is going so well and I am just glad that I have not seen the man that has been stalking me. I really prayed to God and cried out to Him, so I know that this man is not coming back. God isn't going to allow him to.

It's been a couple months since I quit my job and all I can say is that me and my daughter have not wanted for anything. We have everything we need and all my bills are paid on time. Money has just been coming out of nowhere. Whenever I ask God to help me, He always comes through for me and my daughter. Now, I know for a fact that it was Him speaking and telling me that He will provide for me.

I'm just in such a good mood, so I decided to let a few ladies from my church come stay the night at my house. We are always at church, so this should be a way for us to have some type of fun. The night is going great, our conversations lasted for hours. After the talking, we decided to finally go to sleep around 5 in the morning, especially since we had church in the morning. While we were all sleeping in the living room, we began to hear tapping on the window. At first, we didn't really think anything of it, until the tapping continued and had some type of beating pattern. We all woke up and as we looked to the window we had seen a huge shadow. I know it's this man again and all I could do was panic. I can't take this anymore, so I go run to the window and pull the blind back to look out the window and all I had seen was this tall man hop off the side of my porch.

I am so sick and tired of this man harassing me and the police act as if they can't do anything about it. It's like they're waiting for him to hurt me, before they can act. I really thought that this was over and he was not going to bother me anymore. I prayed about it and I thought that the Lord heard my cry! Why would God allow me to go through this? I don't deserve what's happening to me. I just don't know what to do, or who to talk to. No one seems to know how I feel, especially if they never had someone stalk and torment them. I'm afraid all over again and I have to be to church in a few hours. I have to stand up in front of these people and sing praise and worship, while acting as if nothing is wrong with me. Lord, please just give me the strength to handle every situation that I am going through.

It's been a few months and this man Greg has still been harassing me, knocking on my door, peeking in my windows and making it known that he doesn't plan on stopping. But this night, what he did was, by far, the worst thing he could have done.

Me and my daughter were at home by ourselves and I got a call from my sister Lynn, letting me know that she was on her way and she was coming to spend the night. I said, "okay." I'm always happy when someone comes and stays the night with us, because I really hate being alone in this house with my daughter. I got a call from my home girl Donna. She began to ask me what I was doing and I let her know I was just at home with my daughter. She wasn't talking about anything so she said, "okay" and hung up. It's around 12 o'clock in the morning and Lynn just got to my house, we are upstairs in my daughter's room talking. Then, out of nowhere, we heard someone banging on my backdoor. They were banging so hard, that I knew the neighbors could hear them. They banged and banged harder and harder, then a man's voice began to say, "Open up the door Shay, I know you in there by yourself." Now, we knew that it was that man Greg.

My hands began to shake, as I was in so much fear that he was going to break my door down. I quickly reached for my phone and gave it to my sister and said, "Call the police." I was so afraid;

I couldn't speak to them. Right now, all I can do is lock us in the room where we were in, grab my daughter, drop to my knees and start praying that the Lord will protect us. I began to cry hysterically and my daughter was screaming and crying because of the fear of this man coming in. He began to bang on my side windows harder and harder, then out of nowhere it just stopped. I made my sister call my mom and dad and tell them to come over now. Then, while she was calling, we heard the doorbell ring. I was too afraid to leave the room, but I had to see if it was the police.

We all slowly walked down the stairs. At this point, my sister Lynn is crying too. I look out the window, slowly, and it was the police. I quickly opened the door, they looked surprised because of how hysterical my sister and I were. They told us to tell them what happened. I let them know everything about the man, Greg, that has been stalking me and taping on my window for about 7 months now, and tonight, he finally tried to get in. The more I talked, the more I cried. The police seemed sympathetic, yet again, they said that there was nothing they could do, because I did not actually see him. They must catch him on my property and he was not here when they got here.

While the police were leaving, my parents were pulling up. They hurried and got into the house and asked what happened. I let them know and they were not happy at all. They don't want to see their daughter going through anything like this, especially my father. He was so upset, trying to call up my uncles to go and handle this man, but it's not even worth it. My mom really doesn't know what to say, but I know that she is worried about me. They asked if we wanted to come and stay the night with them, but I just said no. I just can't run from my own home. All I know, is that I am going to talk to my housing specialist, as soon as I wake up tomorrow. After they left, Lynn and I went upstairs and locked ourselves in my room and went to sleep.

Lynn left for school and my daughter and I were on our way to talk to someone about what just happened last night. When I got to the building, I asked to speak to my housing specialist and I told them that it was an emergency. Within the next fifteen minutes, she came and called me into her office. She asked why I came today for a visit and I began to tell her everything, starting from when I first moved in my house to Greg stalking me. I also let her know what happened just last night. As I began to explain all I was going through, I could not hold back my tears, they just began to flow.

She let me finish talking and then she began to say that she has good news, "The good news is that they have a program for people who are being harassed or stalked and we provide them with a voucher to help pay for their rent so that they can move and the person who is being harassed is able to break their lease because of the horrifying circumstances and you are qualified for this program." She began to have me fill out a bunch of paper work and by the end of the visit, she gave me a house voucher of $750, that I can now start looking for homes to move into, as soon as possible. All I can say is, "Lord, I thank you. I'm getting out of that house."

I'm still in shock about what just happened last night, so I end up going to talk to my cousin Ti-Ti. If anyone knows how I feel, she knows, because she is always there when that man comes and she is just as afraid as I am. As I'm talking to her and telling her what happened, something told me to ask her if it was her that banged on my door. I don't know why I asked her, because I knew it was Greg, the man that was stalking me and it was a man's voice, but I asked anyways. Suddenly, she looked up at me with a compassionate face and said "Sorry, we all did it." Me being confused, I said, "Yaw did what?" She said, "Me, Lisa, Donna and Bonnie came to your house last night and banged on your doors and windows and Lisa acted like a man and said, 'Open up the door Shay, I know you in there by yourself.'" My heart began to sink to my stomach, as tears began to roll down my face, "Why would you all do something like that, you know what I have been through with this man, why imitate him to torment me." "Sorry Shay, it was a joke we didn't know you was going to call the police and take it so serious." "So, that'swhy Donna called me last night and asked me am I home, so yaw can scare me? All of you were there at least one time, when this man came and you all were scared so why do this to me? You know what, just leave me alone."

How could they do that to me, to my daughter, thank God, that Lynn was there with me. I don't even know who to trust anymore. You don't do things like that to people you love, joke or no joke, that was just plain cruel. I end up leaving and going to talk to some woman of my church. They always understand me and I can cry right on their shoulder. It hurts, but I'm going to get through this. Trouble doesn't last always.

Chapter Eleven

Answered Prayer

    I have been looking everywhere for a house to move into, but I just have not been having any luck finding one. Every house that I have gone to look at is either a home that is disgusting or a house that I would love to move into, but it costs too much. It is so difficult, especially in the timeframe of two months that it requires. At this point in my life, I can honestly say that I just wish that I had a good man in my life. Someone that will protect me and my daughter that will love us and provide for us. I have been single for a long time and I really pray that I meet someone soon. I really need someone that will help me in my time of distress, because this situation with this man, Greg, is really causing me to be afraid. I wish I had someone here to help me. I'm not going to stress about having someone, because if it is meant for me to be in a relationship, it will happen.

    I really think that God heard me when I was saying that I was ready for a relationship, because I just happened to meet this man the other day, his name is Denzel. He is a local rapper in the town and I was looking for an artist to perform at our church for Open Mic night, so I reached out to him. He gladly accepted the offer and then, he suggested that we should do a song together for Open Mic night too. I thought it would be a cool idea, so we began to meet up and practice. Honestly, this man is such a cool dude. He is funny, charming, and he is a gentleman. It's like the more time we spend together, the more we just connect. Our chemistry is crazy! He even gets along well with my daughter. She was a little resistant at first, but suddenly, they became real close and that really is important.

Denzel and I finished our song and it sounds amazing, but that didn't stop us from seeing each other! Meeting him has brought so much light into my world, especially when it felt so dark. His humor makes me feel so joyous and I am so thankful that I met him, at such a difficult time in my life. I feel so comfortable around him and I feel like I can talk to him about anything. I recently told him about my situation with the man that has been stalking me and he immediately said, "You don't have to worry anymore I'm going to protect you." Just hearing those words melted my heart, because I prayed for this. All I wanted was for God to send me someone that will love me and my daughter and protect us. I know that Denzel means what he says.

Denzel began to stay the night with me and I could not be happier. Whenever he is here, I feel so safe and I just know that I am going to be alright. It's just the nights that he is not here that fear consumes me. All I want is for Denzel to come back over. We both want to be with each other and we have been touching on the topic of marriage, so we decided to make it official and move in together. Just knowing that Denzel is going to be here with me and my daughter just brings me so much peace. No one understands the nights that I cried myself to sleep, afraid that this man was going to come and break into my house. I hated locking me and my daughter in the room at night, while we sleep just in case that man was able to somehow get in. Now, I have Denzel and he understands what I have been through and all he cares about is keeping us safe. I know it isn't right to live with a man before marriage, but I can't live in fear anymore. I have been afraid for too long.

Denzel and I have been doing great, but I know it isn't right, because I have been having intercourse with him and we are not married. We want to be married, but we really don't have the funds to make it happen. Every time I go to church and hear the word, I feel awful about the sin that I am in. But, then I think about how I was suffering before I met him and how I am so much happier now that he lives with me. I just don't feel comfortable singing in church while sleeping with a man that am not married to, because I know better. So, I began to just come to church late so that I wouldn't make it to sing praise and worship.

Chapter Twelve

Afraid Of Being Judged

I haven't been feeling like myself lately and my menstrual has not come on yet. One thing I know, is that I am not ready to have another child, especially since I am not married. Denzel and I are in a good place, but he has a baby already and I have a child also. I just hope and pray that I am not pregnant. I'm about to go to the store right now and get a pregnancy test, just to make sure.

I went quickly to the store and now, I'm home nervous about to see what this test says. As I waited for the two minutes to pass, all I can think about was the ridicule and judgment that would be thrown at me if this test was to come up positive. I began to think about the people that would laugh at me and say, "I told you she wasn't as holy as she was claiming to be, up there singing, but sleeping with a man that's not her husband." I just pray this test is negative. I finally reached for the stick and quickly glanced and it was 2 bold lines, it's positive. I am pregnant. This just can't be happening. How am I going to tell Denzel?

I called Denzel up and told him we needed to talk, so we met up a few hours later. I began to say that I have to show him something and I pulled the test out of my purse and said, "I'm pregnant." Surprisingly, he had a smile on his face and said, when I spoke those words, it felt like a fire cracker went off and he began to get excited. Then, he began to say he doesn't know how to feel, because he just had a baby. I can understand how he felt. We both aren't ready for another child, but I'm already pregnant.

It's been about a months and I am still in disbelief that I am carrying another child. Denzel and I were doing well, until we had a little argument and he ended up getting angry and leaving around 11 o'clock at night. I also began spotting last night and I don't know why or if this is normal in a pregnancy. I woke up the next day, really stressed and worried about him leaving so suddenly over such a small disagreement. As the day carried out, I just began to feel these sharp cramps in my stomach, like a menstrual cramp, but probably ten times worse. I laid down and held my stomach, as I began curl up in a ball.

The pain felt unbearable, all I could do was call for my daughter, saying, "Mommy needs your help." I told her to go get me my medication and a juice out of the refrigerator. She quickly handed it to me, so I began to take some painkillers. I don't know what is happening, but I know something must be wrong. After about thirty minutes, the pain began to decrease a little bit, allowing me to make it to the bathroom. When I looked down, while sitting on the toilet, all I seen was blood clots and something that looked like human body tissue. I began to cry, because I think I just lost my baby. I called my doctors and set up an appointment to see what's going on. Then, I called Denzel, but he won't answer any of my calls, because of the small argument we had. I just wish he was here for me. All I want to do is tell him that I lost the baby.

It's been about a week and he finally reached out to me. All I could do was cry and tell him how he wasn't there for me, when I lost the baby. He felt bad for avoiding me, while I was losing the baby. It still hurts that my daughter had to be the one helping me, holding me, telling me that I'm going to be okay and he wasn't there.

We talked it out and I forgave him. I went to the doctors and they confirmed that I did lose the baby. God knows we weren't ready, but it still is sad. I don't feel the same mentally and my body doesn't feel the same either. I've been having migraines everyday now and I don't know what is going on with me. Having a miscarriage really affected me. I even dropped out of college.

It's seems like me and Denzel have gotten a lot closer. He finally met my family and I met his family also. Ever since we lost our baby, he has been saying that he wants another child. All I can say is that I am not ready for another child, because I already had to raise my daughter by myself. I don't want to bring another baby in this world, without being married. All he says is that I don't have to raise a child by myself anymore, because he is here now and he is going to be there to help me. I'm just not convinced, because if you want to have a child with me, why aren't you trying to marry me? I just know how hard it is to raise a child on your own and I don't ever want to go through that again. However, he just keeps trying persuade me to have his child.

All he says, is that he will be the one staying up all night taking care of the baby and I don't have to do anything. But I'm just not ready for another child. That's another big responsibility that I am not ready to deal with. It all sounds good, but honestly a child is such a big responsibility and I don't think he understands that.

Chapter Thirteen

It Just Never Ends

It's been a long night and I'm just ready to go to sleep. My boyfriend and I were just about to go to bed, when something told him to go and look out the window. When he looked out, he saw a man by his car in our drive way and I already knew who it was. First thing he did was throw his clothes on and begin to go look for him, because he ran off when we turned the lights on. He came back about 15 minutes later and said that he couldn't find him anywhere. I told him to just go to bed and he said he couldn't sleep and he was going to watch the house all night while I sleep.

It couldn't be any more than 30 minutes that had passed and he saw Greg running from off our porch. My boyfriend was already dressed, so he quickly ran outside to run after him. But, as he was walking outside, our next-door neighbor was on his way over to our house. My boyfriend stopped to see what he wanted and he asked if that man was looking in our window too, because they just seen him looking in their window. They both decided that they were going to go to his house and give him a beating for coming to their house.

I gave them the address, because it was in my order of protection that the police gave me. They both rode over to his house with bats and metal pipes. When they arrived to the door, they banged and banged and no one answered. That didn't stop them from trying to get at him. They began to go to every window in the whole house and bang on each one. "Open up the door Greg," they said, with a tone that would scare anyone, especially at 3 o'clock in the morning. Suddenly, they see that the door began to open slowly and a little black lady came to the door; she looked scared to death.

"Where is Greg Diss?" Denzel yelled furiously, with a face that would have made anyone scared. "He isn't here, I don't know where he is," the woman said in a quiet, timid voice. Denzel was enraged, knowing that he was not there. "Tell him, the next time he steps a foot anywhere near my woman's house, that's going to be the last day he will be breathing." Then, they walked off and drove back to the house.

Chapter Fourteen

The Unexpected Happens

I don't want any children right now. I'm not ready to take on a whole new responsibility of raising another child, so why do I continue to not use protection with Denzel? Every week, he asks me if I'm pregnant with this grin on his face. He is eager for us to have a baby, but I don't want another child. I really need to get on some sort of birth control, so I won't get pregnant.

Denzel just came back from the store and he has this mischievous look on his face. So, I asked him what's going on. He pulls two pregnancy tests out the bag and says, "Your menstrual didn't come on yet, take these tests." I looked at him in confusion, not understanding how he even knows my menstrual cycle. I took the box and went into the bathroom. Of course, Denzel came right along with me. I followed all the instructions on the box and then, we had to wait for two minutes. We patiently waited, and finally our two minutes were up. Denzel ran to the test first and he looked disappointed. He handed me the test and screamed, "We having a baby!" I quickly looked at the test and it was positive, two lines. Wow, we really are having a baby.

Denzel went upstairs, while I went to sit down and just think. Why didn't I just use protection? I really don't want to have another child right now. I can't go to church and sing in front of everyone, while I am pregnant. So many thoughts were going through my mind.

I went upstairs to the bathroom and I see that Denzel had fixed me a bubble bath with candles everywhere. He came in the bathroom and gave me a kiss and said, "We are really having a baby, I love you." I really feel special and he is so excited. However, I am still stressed that I am carrying a child right now. I was supposed to be married first, not having another child out of wedlock. I don't know what to do.

Going to church has been awkward for me. I don't feel comfortable going, knowing that I am pregnant. I just don't want anyone to ask me to sing. I know that I am not living right and I just can't go before God's people, while I am not living how God wants me to live. I feel so ashamed and disappointed in myself. What will people think, if they find out that I am pregnant? How would they react? I am really perplexed.

Denzel has been taking good care of me. He is always there for me and he makes sure that I am feeling alright. I am thankful for him. He is like the total opposite of my daughter's father. It feels good to know that someone loves you and really wants to have a child with you and that they will do anything to make you happy. He is everything I've always wanted.

I know this is not happening again, I thought to myself while sitting in church. I'm feeling sharp pains all in my stomach, like the pain I felt when I had the last miscarriage. I began to sweat and hold my head down, as the pain began to get more intense by the minute. I quickly texted Denzel and told him to come pick me up. Denzel arrived in 10 minutes, I slowly walked to the car with my daughter. Not trying to draw any attention to myself and the pain I was feeling, I got in the car and started to cry. "I think I am having a miscarriage." Denzel hurried to the house, helped me out the car and took me to the bathroom. I went to look for blood and when I looked down I seen big clots, like the time before.

Denzel looked very disappointed and told me to call the doctors to schedule an appointment to make sure it was a miscarriage. I called and then we just talked. He gave me some pain reliever pills and stood by my side the whole night.

We are at the doctors and they ask me to take a urine test. My test came back a faint positive, showing that I most likely lost the baby. Later, they took my blood work to know for sure. My blood came back and I did indeed have a miscarriage. Honestly, after having two miscarriages back-to-back, I am feeling grief. Now, I am wondering what is wrong with me and why I can't have a baby now. Why do I keep losing my babies? I have so many questions. I just don't understand why I lost another child.

It's been a few weeks and I am not doing that well. Every time I see a baby or watch a baby commercial, I begin to tear up. My heart is so heavy right now and I just don't understand why I lost my babies. I began to get emotional, whenever I see someone that is pregnant. All I can think is, why couldn't I still have my baby? I know I wasn't ready, but I didn't want to have another miscarriage. This is really a difficult time for me right now and I am in deep depression. I just don't know how to handle these emotions.

Chapter Fifteen

For Better Or For Worse

Guess who's planning on getting married soon? Denzel and I! We have been doing well in our relationship and we both feel that it is time to take it to the next level. I mean, why not? We're practically doing everything that married couples would do. I love his son and I'll do anything for him and he feels the same way about my daughter. Why not make it official?

We have been going to marriage counseling with my Pastor and it has really been helpful. One thing we both learned in our session is to put God first, because this is the most successful step to having a great relationship. I can understand why, because when you put God first, you will do the right things by others, especially your significant other. If you have a thought about being unfaithful, the Lord will let you know, that is not the right thing to do. If you and your mate get into a heated argument and you seem to not be able to forgive, Jesus will put it in your heart that you should forgive, so that you may be forgiven. If both partners put God first, relationships can last much longer.

Denzel and I only went to a few counseling sessions, not because we didn't want to continue, but because something had happened with the church. I don't really know too much; all I know is that I received a text saying that we will no longer be at our current church and they will keep us posted. I never would have thought that the church I learned so much from, would be closed. Now what am I to do? Going to church kept me grounded and it helped me to want to do better. One thing I know that I don't want to do is start looking for another church to attend. I loved my church. It was where I felt comfortable. Lord, what is going on?

    Now that we don't have a church anymore, it seems like most of us are all lost. Some people found a new church and others went back to doing all the things they did, before they started going to church. It's just sad how it all happened. I miss going to church and I am also still depressed about losing our baby. Lord, I need answers.

Chapter Sixteen

My Mind Is Made Up

I think I want a baby now! I'm ready! All I keep thinking about is having another child. I wish I didn't lose my baby. I'm ready to try again! When I told Denzel, he was happy to hear me say these things. It seems like that is all he really wants.

I have my own Registered Family Daycare in my home, so I can be at home with the baby and still work. I think this is really what I want to do. It just feels like a piece of me has been lost, since I had a miscarriage and the only way for me to feel complete is if I try to have another child again. Just thinking about me not being able to conceive brings tears to my eyes. I just don't understand why this keeps happening to me. I just wish I had someone to talk to. I want someone that understands what I am going through. I try to talk to Denzel, but he thinks it's all my fault and he would sometimes ask, "Why can't I have a baby?" It makes me feel like something is wrong with me.

At this point in my life, I don't care about what others think of me, I just want to do what is going to make me happy. I know that having another baby will bring me such joy. It will also make my daughter happy and she would love to have someone to play with. My mind is made up. Denzel and I are going to try and have another baby.

It's been almost year, since I had my last miscarriage and we have been trying to have a baby ever since. I don't know what is wrong with me. It just seems like I can't get pregnant anymore. Denzel keeps asking me what's wrong and why aren't I getting pregnant? I don't know why I can't conceive. Every time he asks me that, I just shut down and become withdrawn. It just makes me feel like something is wrong with me. I don't understand why everyone else can have babies without any complications, but I can't even carry out a pregnancy. I'm just thankful that God blessed me with my daughter. At least I already had a beautiful baby girl that I love so much.

Denzel really wants to have another baby, so he began searching the internet on ways to conceive. I guess he came across a site that told him to make sure he has intercourse on my ovulation date. He knows my menstrual cycle like the back of his hand. He knew the exact day that they were referring to. When that day came, all he said to me was, "You're ovulating aren't you?" You already know what came next.

Chapter Seventeen

The Fallout

I wonder if Denzel's plan worked. I would be really shocked, if I was pregnant. I would also be afraid, because I believe that something is wrong with my body, causing me to have miscarriages. I'm going to go and get a test from the store, while Denzel is at work, just to see if I am pregnant.

I'm so nervous to take this test. I am sure that it is going to come out negative, but I'm just going to take it anyways. I began to follow the instructions on the box and now it is time to wait for the results. I waited for the two minutes to be up and I grabbed the stick, full of curiosity. I took a deep breath, as I slowly looked at the results and there, I had seen two bold blue lines. I'm pregnant! All I could do was smile and think of a special way to share the news with Denzel.

I got a special card and on the inside of it, I wrote, "We are pregnant," with the positive pregnancy test in the envelope. I put it in the drawer in the kitchen and sent him a message, telling him to check the drawer. When he got home from work, he looked in the drawer and he found what he was looking for. He looked at me and said "You're really pregnant?" I smiled vigorously with a feeling of joy and said, "Yes, we are pregnant!" He didn't say anything. He just kind of seemed shocked, as if he thought it wouldn't have really happened. He wasn't acting happy like he was when I was pregnant before. I don't understand what is wrong with him, right now.

I don't know if it is the hormones, but Denzel and I have not been seeing eye to eye. It seems like, suddenly, he has this attitude. It is Christmas day and Denzel, my daughter, and I were supposed to go and spend the day at his mother's house. I was ironing my clothes and out of nowhere, we just began to argue about nothing. I can't even remember what we were mad about, that's how petty it was. Later that day Denzel went to his mother's house, to help her pick people up, while me and my daughter went to visit my family, before we headed to see Denzel's family.

I was at my mother's house for a couple hours and out of nowhere I get a text message from Denzel saying, "Don't come out here to my mom's, if you are going to have an attitude. People can feel your bad energy." Did he just text me on Christmas day and tell me not to come and spend this holiday with his family, because I have an attitude? He didn't want me to come with him in the first place. We didn't even really have a big argument and it was not even serious. I can't believe him. He is really acting different. I'm not even going to go over there, if I'm not wanted. I'll spend Christmas with my family.

It's almost one o'clock in the morning and he is still not here. He didn't even come home on Christmas night. Holidays are important to me and I can't believe we spent this one apart. To make matter worse, I'm extra emotional, because my hormones are everywhere from this pregnancy. Why wouldn't he come home? What is going on with him?

Ding Dong, Ding Dong. My doorbell is ringing off the hook. I already know who it must be. I come open the door and it is Denzel. All I can do is look at him with disappointment and say, "It is nine o'clock in the morning. Where were you all last night?" He quickly said he stayed the night at his mother's house, because I was not here to open the door for him last night. "So, why didn't you call me to say you were on your way?" I said. He said, "My phone died and my mom phone was dead too, so we couldn't call you." He just doesn't sound like he makes sense, but I'm not going to stress myself out. I'm not going to let anything make me lose my baby, again.

One of the worst feelings in a relationship is being with someone and they don't come home at night. They don't call you to let you know where they are at, or ask if you are okay. Them being gone all night, allows all kind of concerning thoughts to roam through your mind, especially if they left the house while they were angry. I just don't know what his problem is. I just can't let his actions bother me and I must stay stress free to carry this baby to full term.

It's been a couple days, since Denzel didn't come home that night and I can just feel the tension between us. We were talking about his other child and I began to ask questions about his relationship with his child's mother. I just simply asked him how they interact with each other. The only reason why I asked this question is because I have never been around them. He kind of keeps that part of his life private. However, he must know every detail about me and my daughter's father.

I guess he got upset about me asking him about her, because he began to get an attitude, saying that I am jealous of their relationship. I was kind of confused, because this is the same man that told me he hated her and that they don't like each other. "Now suddenly yaw have a relationship, but you tell me you don't even want me to speak one word to my daughter's father." Denzel's face began to frown up as if he was pissed, because I am questioning him. He came in my face and looked me in my eyes and just said, "Shay fuck you."

In complete shock, I screamed furiously and said, "You can leave then." After that, he said one of the worst things anyone could ever say to me, something that caused my heart to break all over again. "I understand why that nigga Terrell left you, while you were pregnant!" Denzel shouted. If he never said anything that hurt me before, this is one of the worst things he could have ever said. Why would someone use that very thing to hurt you all over again? All I could do was break down and cry.

He began to pack up all his things and he called someone to come get him. As he walked out of the door, I realized that this is another pregnancy I have to go through alone.

Honestly, all of this could have been avoided. There was no reason for him to go off on me the way he did. All I did was ask him a question that I wanted to know the answer to and he just treated me like my feelings didn't matter. Lord, please give me strength and please heal my broken heart.

Chapter Eighteen

Something Wasn't Right

It's been about two weeks and I haven't heard anything from Denzel. Today is my doctor's appointment and I have to get a pelvic exam to check for anything that might complicate my pregnancy. The doctor seemed nice and she was asking me about the father of the baby. I wish I could have told her the truth and told her what was going on right now. I just wish I could talk to someone. But, I just told her good things about him and how we planned this pregnancy. The visit went by smooth. I just wish he was there with me.

It's been a few days since I have been to the doctors and I am just lying in the bed thinking about a lot of things. Suddenly, my phone rings and I pick it up quickly, wondering who it is. "Hello?" I said. "Hello, this is Dr. Young from the midwifery group." I didn't know why she was calling me, especially since I just had an appointment. "I was calling to tell you that you have tested positive for Chlamydia," she said. "Chlamydia?" I said confused. "I'm sorry, you should just talk to your boyfriend, and I will send you two prescriptions to the pharmacy for the both of you. So, that you both can be treated." "Wait, I don't understand, how do you get chlamydia, he cheated on me?" I said. "The only way you can contract this infection is through sexual contact, such as sperm or secretion from a vagina," she said. "I'm sorry again that you have to go through this, please just talk with your partner." "Thank you so much Dr. Young and have a nice day."

Tears just began to flow down my face. I can't believe the man that I am in love with has been cheating on me. I can't believe he gave me a sexually transmitted disease. I have never in my life had a disease. I am in total disbelief at this moment. How could he do this to me? No wonder why he has been acting different and treating me real dirty. Now I see why, because he has been seeing someone else. His phone isn't even on right now, so I can't tell him over the phone. I guess I am just going to have to inbox him on Facebook, the social media website that he is always on.

"Hit me up ASAP", that's what I sent to his inbox. Suddenly, he writes me back quickly and it said, "I want nothing to do with you." How could he say he wants nothing to do with me? I'm carrying his child that he wanted me to have. You know what, I'm about to write him exactly what's on my mind. I was trying to be nice and give him his medication, so that he isn't still infected, but he just pissed me off. So, I wrote, "I have to give you something from the Doctor. Honestly, I'm not with the kiddy games. I'm a grown woman and I don't have time to play with you! We both have to handle this situation as two adults. It's not the time to be acting like a child. You don't have to have anything to do with me, but you purposely got me pregnant and you wanted this baby, so don't try to act like it don't exist now. You were the one that looked up my ovulation date and got me pregnant, but now you want to say you don't want anything to do with me. God got me, I'm not worried about you and all I'm worried about is this child that we both wanted. And you really need to reevaluate yourself and find out why you purposely get a woman pregnant and then, say you don't want anything to do with them. It might be a generational curse from your father. You should pray about it, because you do have a relationship with the Lord. All you have to do is get this stuff from the doctors. You can even have your mom come get it or I can drop it off."

He responded by writing, "I want nothing to do with you! And I would be wrong if I say you need to reevaluate yourself and find out why you get pregnant by niggas, to keep them. Maybe that's a generational curse." He doesn't even make any sense, we both wanted this baby and he was the one that did all the searching on-line to have one. Let me write him back. "Why would I want a cheater? I'm good, you can stay with the slut you cheated on me with that gave you chlamydia," I typed furiously. I know he is going to be mad that I found out he cheated and I know he didn't think he had a disease. I didn't want to tell him like this, but he really is just trying to hurt me. I just can't take it.

What he wrote back to me was the dumbest statement ever, I guess he is embarrassed. He wrote, "Or them niggas that you were having sex with, we all know how you church girls is. It's funny, because in your life, I believe, innocent you, been around the block more than me." I knew he was just making up things now, because he was caught, but the next thing he wrote me made me feel sad. He wrote, "And, stop trying to get on my mom's good side, because she just sent me a message saying me and my old girlfriend Taya (her favorite she would say), should go on a date." I thought his mom and I were cool, but I guess not. I can't believe she is really trying to have him go on a date with his ex-girlfriend, while we were together and I am carrying his child. I responded by saying, "The best of luck to you and Taya. All I care about is you taking care of the baby you wanted! I don't care about anything else and I don't need to know who you date. That's none of my business."

Honestly, I just can't believe it ended up like this. It's like once you get pregnant, these men just switch up. I just don't understand. I never thought that Denzel would do me like this. I'm just going to pray and ask God to have mercy on him. The Lord loves me and I know it hurts Him to see me go through this. I know that the Lord got my back, so I'm not worried. It hurts, but I'm about to pray, read my Bible, snuggle up with my daughter and go to sleep.

I'm feeling better, after what happened yesterday. I am happy I prayed and gave the situation to God. I looked on the internet and I see that I have a new message from Denzel. I don't even want to look at it. I don't have time for the drama today. I opened the message cautiously, not knowing what to expect. It read, "I'm better than what I wrote, and I know that God is still working on me. But, what do you need from me? Because, I am not running from my responsibilities, I didn't with my son and I won't now! I take back the hurtful things I spoke. Even though our bridge is burned, there is no need for me to be nasty. I am better than that!"

I was shocked to read these words, I am just thankful that I gave the situation to the Lord. He hears my prayers. I joyfully wrote him back and said, "Thank you, I appreciate that. The doctor just needs me to give you the medication and just speak with you, that was it. I just wish that you would try to make it to the doctor appointments, because I just can't go through a whole pregnancy by myself again. I don't ever want you to think that I'm trying to trap you. I'm fine with us not being together. I was thinking about getting an abortion, because of the way that you were treating me. I didn't want to feel the pain that I went through before. But, I honestly heard God loud and clear and He said, "How dare you try to get rid of this child that I have formed in you, after you were so sad that you had miscarried. How dare you?" So, I am not trying to keep our child because of you, I am keeping this baby, because it is right."

Chapter Nineteen

Welcome Back

It's been a while and Denzel and I are not on talking terms. He missed the baby's first ultrasound and I am really hurt by it. I asked him if he was going to go, but he just said no. I just feel that it shouldn't matter if we are together or not, you should still be there to make sure everything is fine with your baby. I really don't want to go through this pregnancy alone. I just wish we could just work something out.

I just got a call from Denzel and he wants to talk to me in person. We need to talk about a lot and I would love to show him the ultrasound pictures. I also want to know who he cheated on me with, when, where and how. I want to know every detail. I still can't believe he did that to me, but I am going to hear him out and hopefully everything works out.

Ding dong! I hurry to the door with anticipation, because I can't wait to hear what he has to say. I open the door and Denzel comes walking in. It felt like we hadn't seen each other in months and you can just feel the tension in the room. I looked at him and said, "So what happened, who did you cheat on me with?"

"You know what, I am going to tell you the truth. My homeboy and I were at a tattoo party and we were all drinking.

You know I don't drink alcohol, but I decided to drink that night, I got so drunk, I just start feeling myself. My boy was in the other room and they left me in the back room with this tall, overweight, dark skinned girl. I don't even remember her name. I guess that liquor had me feeling bold, so I just ask her to give me oral sex. She said no at first, but I just kept asking her and she just ended up doing it. I wish I would have never did that and I am sorry. I'm missing out on everything, your stomach is getting bigger, I want to be around my family and I want to be here with you. I am sorry, I love you and I won't do that again."

All I could do was cry, "You really hurt me, you are going to have to do a lot to get my trust back, Denzel." Then, he says, "I am willing to do whatever it takes to get your trust back," while kissing me on my forehead. I forgive him, but it will take time to trust him again.

Denzel has been doing everything possible to gain my trust back. He keeps his phone unlocked and he keeps all his social media profiles open. Whenever he is gone for too long, he calls me to tell me what is going on, so that I don't think he is doing anything wrong. We are in a good place. I'm happy I gave him another chance and it feels good to have him here, while I am carrying his baby.

Chapter Twenty

What's Done In The Dark

Will Come To The Light

    I finally let my whole family know that I was pregnant. I told my mom a couple months ago, but I didn't tell anyone else. I should tell everyone now, because my birthday is coming up in a couple days and they're all going to see that my stomach is bigger anyway. When I told my dad the news, all he said was, whatever decision I make, he will support me. When I told another family member, they said that I should get rid of the baby, because me and Denzel are always breaking up and making up. Regardless of what anyone says, I am still going to keep this baby that God blessed me to carry.

    Guess what today is! It's my 24th birthday and I am so excited to see all my friends and family. My dad ordered a lot of pizza and wings for everyone to eat and we all just had a good time dancing and enjoying each other's company. I felt even happier to have Denzel there, right by my side.

The party went well, I got plenty of good gifts and a good amount of money from everyone. I'm thankful that I have a wonderful family and great friends. My grandmother and grandfather even came and had a good time. I love my family with all my heart and I am blessed to have a family that is so close to each other.

I think that I am going to go to the Casino with my mom and my cousin today, since it is still my birthday weekend. I might have some luck. The Casino is about 30 minutes away and I am probably going to be gone for a while. So, I told Denzel he can just take my car for the day and do whatever he must do, until I get back in town. He was fine with that idea. He dropped me off at my mom's and we headed out to the casino to have some fun.

Denzel is at work and I don't know why, but something just told me to check his social media messages. He would usually let me see all his messages on his phone, but I never had his password, therefore I couldn't check his page if he wasn't the one showing it to me. However, he didn't know that I read one of the messages he sent to his cousin and he gave her his password.

So, I'm just going to look at his page, just because something is telling me too. I know I'm not going to find anything, but I just want to look. I log onto his Facebook social media account and it lets me in. Yes! This is the right password! I just go straight to his messages and I see about 6 different conversations, with 6 different women. I go through each message and I read them all. One message was to some girl that he was asking to give him sexual pleasure, because she promised she would one day. He was basically trying to have sex with one of these girls yesterday, while he was driving my car and while I was at the Casino.

All the girls he wrote were basically brushing him off and didn't want anything to do with him. But, there was one girl named Biggs, whose messages stood out to me. The only thing the message said was, "you can come now." All the other messages were deleted and by the time she wrote him that yesterday, we were already in the house together. Who is this girl and what messages did they write to each other, before he deleted their conversation? I was curious to know who this girl is. I went and looked at her social media page and when I saw who it was, I couldn't believe my eyes. She was brown skinned, tall, very over weight, young and just not someone he'd seem to be attracted to. I didn't know her, but I couldn't believe that he would cheat on me with her. I don't have anything against bigger women. We all come and different shapes and sizes and we are all beautiful in our own way. It's just that Denzel would always say that he doesn't like big girls. He would always make jokes about them, but now suddenly, he is messing with all big girls. I'm just confused.

I'm about to find out the truth, I must know what is going on between the two of them. I must figure out a way to write her, while he is at work and make her believe that he is talking to her from his page. I have to get another opinion on this, so I'm going to ask my little brother what I should do. He would know.

I told him everything and he said, "If you want to know what they were going to do just ask one question, are you going to give me head or nah?" I debated if I should write her from his page and ask her that, but I did it anyway. She quickly replied, "No because you cum too fast when I do" I can't believe this teenager has had sex with my man. I must find out more. So, I wrote, "Where do you want to do it at?" "My place, I guess," she said. I couldn't believe this girl was going to have sex with my man. So, I decided to write back and say, "I can't do this no more, I don't want to hurt my girlfriend and we have a baby on the way." She must have been furious, when she read that message, because she wrote back saying, "I can't believe you have a baby on the way. What does your girlfriend have to do with us? I can't believe you are saying this?" I wrote back, "You knew I had a girlfriend in the first place, so why are you so mad?" She said, "I know you had a girlfriend, but I didn't know that I would catch feelings for you. You were everything I wanted. You were hood, but still sweet. I really was feeling you." I just wrote her and said, "Stop writing me, I'm with my girlfriend now. I don't want you."

Now, I must delete this whole conversation, because I don't even want him to know that I have his password. I just can't believe he has still been cheating on me. I really wish I did not have to go through this, while I am pregnant. I really don't need this stress on me, while I am carrying this baby. I swear, if I knew he was doing all this dirt, before I got pregnant, I would have been left him. Now that I found this out, I just decided to look at every message. I don't care if it was a message from his mother, I'm still going to read it.

I just happened to read some messages from him and his best friend and I went all the way back to their messages from Christmas. Yes, this past Christmas, when he ended up not coming home that night. I was reading and Denzel wrote that he just had sex with stank, dirty Ash from the North side. I couldn't believe what I was reading. So, he told me he stayed at his moms on Christmas, but he spent Christmas night with another woman and all her kids. Then, he calls her stank and dirty. Really? He chose her over me. What is wrong with this man?

This is just too much to take in right now. I have never felt so betrayed in my life. This is the man that I thought I was going to marry. The man that I brought my daughter around. The man that I thought was a gift from God, but he turned out to be everything I despised. I don't even know what to say. A part of me wants to just keep it in, until I have this baby and another part of me just wants to kick him out and never see him again.

Chapter Twenty-One

His Lies Caught Up To Him

    I already wrote the girl Biggs from my personal page, as myself, and asked her for her number. I texted her and told her that I saw the messages from her and Denzel. She wrote me back and acted like she never met him and she doesn't know who Denzel is. I know that she knows him. Why is she acting like she doesn't? What type of female is this? I guess she is a typical homewrecker?

    He just got in from work and I don't even know how to approach him. I am trying to keep my cool, but something in me just wants to go crazy on him. I wait, until I put my daughter to sleep and I come back downstairs, where he was and I just simply asked him who Biggs is. He looked puzzled, acting, as if he didn't understand who I was talking about. "Who is she?" I said quietly with tears coming down my face. He remained quiet and began to walk up to me trying to hold me. "Get off me!" I screamed. I didn't want to say much more, because I didn't want him to know how I found out about her. I went upstairs to cool off and I ended up checking his messages again. "Yo, yo, yo", he wrote three times to her, while I was upstairs. She quickly wrote back, "Chill, I didn't snitch on you!" Little do they both know, I am reading all their messages. I can't believe how sneaky he is and how much of a homewrecker she is.

I didn't bring her up again, so he ended up coming to bed and falling asleep. I just started thinking and I couldn't sleep at all. It's about 3:00 in the morning and I decided to write her again from his page acting like him, because I want to know everything. "My girlfriend just kicked me out and I don't care about anything anymore, tell her the truth about us." My text message notification instantly went off and it was from her. She is about to tell me the whole truth, because she thought he told her to.

By time I grabbed my phone and put my passcode in, Denzel hopped up out of his sleep and grabbed my phone out of my hands and ran into the bathroom and locked it. "Give me my phone!", I yelled. All I kept hearing was my phone's text notification continuously going off. I know she was telling me everything. I can't believe he has my phone right now. How did he even wake up out of his sleep like that? I banged and banged on the door and he would not let me in. Almost an hour went by and he opens the door and throws me my phone.

I hurry and look for my text messages and the only thing I have from her, was a text saying that Denzel and her mutual friend were writing from their page and he was trying to mess with my head. Does this little girl really think I am stupid? She just told me that she doesn't know Denzel. Now, suddenly, she does and she knows his friends too. Denzel really must have put a spell on this girl, because she will do whatever he says. She is the true definition of a "side chick." He doesn't even know he messed with the wrong one now.

Honestly, I'm just trying to keep my stress levels down and I'm not even going to say anything to Denzel yet. He thinks that he just pulled a fast one over on me. I got something for him. I decided to go talk to my sister Lynn and her boyfriend. I let them know everything that was going on, I just needed someone to vent to. Just talking to the people that love me makes me realize that I don't deserve to be dealing with this stress, especially while I am pregnant. I already made my decision, Denzel must go.

I had them come to the house with me, once Denzel got out of work. I walked in the house and looked Denzel in the eyes and said, "Make sure your stuff is out of my house before I get back." He looked disappointed, realizing that his little lies didn't get through to me. "But, I don't have nowhere to go, I'm comfortable here" he said. "Go live with your best friend, or your mother, that's not my problem," I said. Then, I walked out the house and went to my mother's house for a few hours, until he could get all his things.

I got back to the house and he was leaving with his things. We didn't say much to each other. There's really nothing to talk about. He couldn't tell me the truth and he wanted to cover up his lies. That's just something I can't deal with. I'm disappointed that we are broken up, again. I am really hurt and we were supposed to find out what we are having in a few days. I got to do what I have to do though. I can't allow him to just treat me any way.

Chapter Twenty-Two

The Struggle

I can't believe how bad it is outside. Last night's snow storm brought about two feet of snow and I have to be to the doctor's in an hour. Let me hurry up and get my daughter and I dressed, so that I can shovel this driveway to make it to my appointment.

We are finally ready to go, so I leave my daughter in the house, while I go to shovel. As I shoveled the driveway, I began to get emotional. It felt like it was below zero outside. My back is killing me, my hands are numb and this is just not fair. No pregnant woman should have to shovel a whole driveway by herself, in the freezing cold. Tears began to flood my eyes, as I continued to shovel. It seemed like, the more I shoveled, the more snow would come. Times like this make me wish that I had Denzel here to help me.

I did the best that I could do shoveling. I grabbed my daughter and put her in the car and began to back out of my driveway. If I thought that my day couldn't get any worse, it did. I am trying to back out, but my car gets stuck. I guess I didn't shovel the end of the driveway that well. I am already going to be late for my appointment, this can't be happening right now. I went to go and get my shovel again and I tried to shovel around the car more, so, I could pull out, but nothing is working. I just don't know what to do. I have been trying to get out for about half an hour now, and I missed my appointment. I am so frustrated. Suddenly, this man comes out from across the street and asks me if I need help. I graciously said, "Yes" then, he came over and pushed my car, while I backed it out. I am so thankful that this man helped me, I thanked him and I drove off with tears in my eyes.

Before he came and helped me, I felt so alone, like no one cared about me. People kept driving by, walking by and not asking if I needed any help. This man cared enough to come and see if I needed help.

I couldn't make it to the doctors, so I just dropped my daughter off at school and rescheduled the appointment. In this appointment, they will tell us the sex of the baby. Hopefully, Denzel will come. I haven't talked to him, since I kicked him out. Even though we are not together, I still want him to be there, so that we can find out what we are having together.

Denzel isn't answering any of my phone calls, I don't understand why he is acting like I am the one that did something wrong, when he is the one that cheated on me. Regardless of anything we are dealing with, I still want him to come to the ultrasound. Since he isn't answering my calls, I will just write him a message on social media.

"Are you going to still come to the doctor appointment Monday? I just want to give you the chance to come see what you are having and I don't want to take this day away from you, regardless of what we are going through. You still deserve to experience the blessing of finding out if you are a having a son or a daughter! It is okay if you choose not to, but please let me know your decision ASAP, just in case I need to have someone else come with me?" He read the message, but he never replied. What is wrong with him?

Tomorrow is the day. I can't wait to find out what I am carrying, I am so excited. Denzel still has not gotten in touch with me and it really hurts. I am going to write him one last time. "So, I guess you are reading your messages and not replying. I guess it is a no! Okay, you can't say I was ever trying to keep you away, even though I'm hurt by this whole situation, I'm trying to stay mature and allow you to find out what sex is the baby and not regret that you didn't come. At least I tried and I gave you the opportunity, but you rejected it. Just remember that you are not hurting me for not coming. You are the only one that is not benefiting from missing the ultrasound and you will be the one that regrets it. When you come to your senses, it will be too late and you will miss everything you wanted to experience. I really don't want that to happen, you should be there regardless of how you feel, concerning me." I am done trying, I am about to tell my sister to come with me to find out. At least, I can always depend on my family to be there.

Chapter Twenty-Three

The Reveal

Today is the day! I am going to find out what I am carrying. I am hoping for a girl, but whatever I am having, I will be thankful, if it is healthy. I am kind of disappointed, because Denzel was reading the messages, but never responded to me. I just never thought he would treat me this way. I guess you just never really know someone.

We are in the ultrasound room and I am in so much anticipation. As I am lying on the table, the ultrasound technician put the warm gel on my stomach and began to press a small handheld device against my belly. She began to show me my baby's little hands and feet. Everything was just perfect, the way a baby should be. My heart is filled with so much joy. I have a living, healthy baby inside of me. After miscarrying back to back, all I can do is feel blessed that my baby is okay.

"Would you like to know the sex of the baby?", the technician said. "Yes, I would," I said with excitement. "Well if you look right here you can see that", she paused. "It's a Boy!" she said ecstatically. All I could do was smile. What am I going to do with a little boy? I am such a girly girl. It doesn't even matter, I am going to love my baby! I hurried to my mother's house and let her know the big news. She was so happy.

I am happy also. I just feel disappointed that I couldn't experience that moment with the father of my child. We both wanted this baby, so that we could experience this together. But, yet again, I am having another child, with another man and I'm going through this all by myself. I dread going to these appointments and seeing other pregnant woman with their husbands or boyfriends right by their side. I just feel like I have been abandoned, left alone to go through this all by myself. Hopefully Denzel will come to his senses.

I still haven't heard from Denzel to tell him the big news. I wanted to tell him in person, but I guess I will just message the ultrasound picture to him. Honestly, I wish I would have never found out that he was cheating on me. I wish that we could just work things out, so that he can be here for me during this pregnancy. I cry so much about how he is acting towards me. I don't want to stress too much and end up losing my baby. I just want to work it out.

Chapter Twenty-Four

Rekindle The Flame

Guess whose birthday it is today? My baby girl, she is turning 5 years old and I'm so excited to see her enjoy her day today. I haven't really talked to Denzel, but today he decided to pop up over my house and give my daughter some money for her birthday. That was sweet, but we still are not on good terms. We didn't even really speak, it was just awkward. We really need to get it together.

My daughter had a great birthday and she received everything that she wanted. I have to give thanks to my mother for helping me, whenever it comes to my daughter. She will pay for her party, get her gifts and help me with anything. It is hard raising a child, while her father is in prison and my mom understands that. I swear, I love her so much and I don't know what I would do without her. She is a true blessing to my daughter and I.

It's been a couple of weeks, since I have seen Denzel, but he has been trying to get back on good terms with me. He is beginning to call to check up on me and he tries to tell me that he loves me. I just can't say it back to him, because I am still hurt from all he has done. I wish we could get back together and make this relationship work, but I just can't trust him. I'm just wondering if being with him would be easier, than being apart and going through this pregnancy alone.

I just wish that all my feelings for Denzel would go away. But they are still as strong as they were, before I was hurt. He has done so many things to hurt me, yet he still has my heart, why? He doesn't deserve a woman like me. And, I don't deserve to be treated the way that he has been treating me.

He says that he wants his family back and that he wants to be with me to help me during this pregnancy. A part of me believes him and a part of me doesn't. We have not been with each other for some months now, maybe he has come to his senses. Maybe he realizes that being here with me is better than being out in the streets, messing with random women.

I know everyone is probably thinking that I am crazy, but I decided to give Denzel another chance. He has been doing everything possible to make me happy and make up for the things that he did. I love him and I know that he loves me too. I am very pleased that we can make it work for our family. Even though we haven't been together most of my pregnancy, I am still grateful that he is here now, toward the end.

We have begun planning for the baby shower and I am so excited. I want to arrange it to be everything I ever wanted. I couldn't do much for my first baby shower with my daughter, because I was not financially able to. But, now that I have the money to do what I desire, I am going to make this a day to remember.

Denzel sprained his ankle and he is now out of work for a while. We are together all the time now and I am enjoying spending this time with him. The only crazy part is, I am seven months pregnant and I have to help him do everything, from putting his socks on, his shoes on, helping him get in the car, helping him shower and even more than that. After all this man put me through, I am still here for him, if he needs me. I just wonder if he would do the same for me.

I finally could get Denzel to come to a doctor's appointment with me and I let my daughter come too. It felt good having them with me. I wish he could have made it to an ultrasound appointment to see the baby, but it's too far in the pregnancy to get anymore. At least he could hear the baby's heartbeat. Once he heard it, he said that it instantly brought tears to his eyes. I'm just pleased that he experienced that moment with me.

One of my favorite singers, Lauryn Hill, is coming to town and I am so excited. Denzel went and bought us some tickets, so we are going tonight to enjoy ourselves. This is why I fell in love with him. He can be so sweet, at times. We really had a good time. It felt good to be somewhere with my man, not arguing or fighting and just enjoying each other's company. Just being together feels right. I hate when we are having problems. Hopefully, this will last a long time.

Chapter Twenty-Five

He Switched Up

It has been about a month and Denzel's injury has healed, so he is now going back to work. Ever since he has been back on his feet, everything just seems different. We barely spend time together now, let alone get physical with each other. My hormones are everywhere. My body is going through so many changes right now, all I want is to be shown love from Denzel. I am just craving that intimacy that we use to have. All he does is come in from work, get on the internet and then says he is going to his brother's house around the corner. I don't know why, suddenly, there is this big disconnect between the both of us.

"Can you rub my feet, they are so swollen and they are aching," I said with desperation. "No, have your daughter rub them for you," he stated in a very sarcastic way. Is he serious right now? I'm not even going to respond to him. I don't know what his issue is, but I'm just going to go upstairs with my daughter. After I have taken care of him the whole time his ankle was messed up, he can't even rub my feet. Wow, I just can't believe him. I wonder, what is it now?

My daughter is put to bed and it's getting late, I still haven't talk to Denzel, after he wouldn't rub my feet. Let me go see what he is doing. I went downstairs and all I see is him lying on the couch surfing the internet on his phone. "Are you coming to bed?" I asked. "I'm going to sleep down here tonight," he said. I walked away feeling disappointed. My mind is already jumping to conclusions. He is probably writing females again, trying to have intercourse with them. He did change his password, so I don't know what he is doing. Plus, he barely touches me, something isn't right.

It's been about a month and Denzel has not slept in our bed once. He always gives the lame excuse, "I fell asleep on the couch." Now, I'm suspicious of everything. I thought we were making progress, but I see we aren't. If I ask him to touch me in any kind of way, just asking him to rub my back, because of the pressure from the baby, he will say no. All he does all day is be on his phone. What is on his phone can be that important, that he is ignoring the one he supposedly loves? I just want some affection from him, but he is acting as if I don't matter.

I feel like he is cheating again and his attention is somewhere else when it should be on me. Now, I have to question him. Matter of fact, I don't even know if he is really going to work, when he says he is. I can't trust this man at all.

"Where were you? I thought you get off work at 3:00 and it is 6 now, where were you?" "I was at my brother house, I just went there straight after work," he said. "Why weren't you answering your phone? What if something happened or what if I needed the car?" "Shay my phone was in the car" "Next time, answer my phone calls and let me know what is going on"

I know he was mad at me for questioning him like that, but guess what, I don't care. He is up to something and I can't trust him. So, whenever I feel something isn't right, I am going to speak on it as soon as possible.

"So, are you sleeping downstairs again tonight," I said. "I don't know" "Why don't you sleep with me anymore or even touch me. What is going on, let's talk" "I don't want to talk, I'm tired," he said, while he was looking in his phone. "How are you tired, but you can be on your phone all day," I said. "Man, stop talking to me, I don't want to talk." Did he just say he doesn't want to talk? I am trying to resolve whatever issue there is between us, but obviously, he is not. Lord, please just give me the strength to have a healthy delivery. I am going to go upstairs and try to remain stress free. I can't understand why this man is acting the way he is, but I'm just going to pray about it.

Recently, I have been crying out for attention from Denzel. I would stay at my mother's house all day, until about midnight. I would come home and see him lying on the couch, hoping he would ask where I have been, or why I am coming in so late. At least, if he would ask any of these questions, I would feel that he still cares. But, I get nothing, I walk in the house, he looks at me and then, he goes right back to getting on his phone. This is not him. He would have called to see where I was at and when I am coming home, before. Now that I am at the end of my pregnancy, I would have thought he would be more concerned about what is going on with me. I could have had the baby or been hurt and he would have never known. It really hurts my feelings and I often find myself tearing up, because of how he is acting towards me. But, one thing I know is that I am going to be alright.

Today is our baby shower and I am excited to see all my family and friends. My friends from high school, Yalonda and

Marra, even showed up. I was so happy to see them. The place looks beautiful and I am feeling beautiful on this day. Of course, Denzel and I are not that happy, but it's time to put the fake smile on and act like everything is just perfect. When his mind and heart can't be with me. My heart and mind is with him, but it takes two people to make a relationship work. At least we are here together, it feels good to have the father of your child here with you.

Chapter Twenty-Six

Unexpected Blessing

"Owww!" all I could do was scream. "What's wrong, you about to have the baby?" "Yes, go get the bags" It's 7 o'clock in the morning and out of nowhere, the sharpest contraction came and I knew it was time. This pain is like 10 times worse, than the pain I felt having my daughter. Denzel hurried up and got me and my daughter in the car. All I could do was keep screaming, it felt like the baby was going to come out, right in the car. He rushed, ran red lights, didn't stop at stop signs and we made it to the hospital quick.

He hurried and got me a wheel chair and the nurses came out and brought me in, while Denzel parked the car. The staff at the hospital asked me my name, but I couldn't even talk, until the contraction was over, the pain was unbearable. Now, they are asking for my insurance card, I can't believe this, can I please just get some medication? They took me to the room to change my clothes, so that they can check my cervix and while I was painfully changing, the unthinkable happened.

I felt so much pressure in my pelvis and the pain increased greatly. Next, it just felt like the baby dropped down, it felt like something broke. I looked down and blood began to run down my leg, my water just broke. I walk out the bathroom to look for a nurse and I see some people laughing at me, because my clothes are halfway off. They began to yell and say, "Someone needs help in here!" Quickly, a midwife comes and helps me get into a hospital bed. She quickly checks my cervix and says, "You are fully dilated" I ask, "Can I get some medication to help with the pain?" She says, "It's too late"

About a second later, I felt the worst pain ever and the pressure in my pelvis was unbearable. "I have to push!" I yelled. I pushed my hardest and I felt my baby's body coming out, I pushed even harder and he popped out, so quickly. They put my baby boy on me and all I could do was feel at ease. My baby made it, he is alive, beautiful, and strong. "You did great", the midwife said.

"Where is my boyfriend? Where is my daughter?" I asked the nurses. "Can someone please go and get him?" I can't believe he missed the birth of our son, because he was parking the car. That is how fast I had the baby, we got to the hospital at 7:24 am and I had the baby at 7:37 am. They finally brought Denzel and my daughter in and they were astonished. No one could believe how fast I had the baby. He came in just in time to cut the umbilical cord. Now, I have to push out the placenta. They weighed him and he is 6 pounds and 18 ½ inches long.

I am still having contraction, even though I already had the baby. This pain is no joke. I can't even feed my baby, I am in so much pain and I feel like I am about to throw up. I, finally, could get some medication for the pain and I feel a lot better. Now, I can hold my baby. I picked him up and all I can do was smile. He is perfect from his head to his toes, I am so in love. This is what I have prayed for. It feels so good to hold him and he is healthy. This is really our miracle baby.

I let my daughter hold the baby a little in her arms and I can tell that she was a little sad. Especially, since she had to leave and stay with my mother, until I get out the hospital. I would never want my daughter to feel unimportant, just because I have a new baby, so I am going to do my best to make her feel comfortable about this new transition.

Everyone has been coming to the hospital and showing us love, my pastor even came and said congratulations. I couldn't be happier; Denzel is here for me. Whenever I am hungry, he gets me food, whenever I need anything, he is there and I appreciate him. Almost two years ago, I kept losing my babies. So, to now be at the hospital, holding a beautiful baby boy, I couldn't feel more blessed and I will forever thank the Lord for this little gift.

We are finally home from the hospital and it feels so good to be able to hold my baby boy. I couldn't ask for anything more, I have my princess and my prince and I love them both the same. My body is drained from not getting much sleep, because of the baby. But, I don't even mind, I wanted my baby so bad and I got exactly what I wanted. Plus, I know what to expect now, I been through this phase before and I know that it will get easier, with time.

As far as Denzel and I go, we still don't have any type of intimacy. It kind of just feels like we are roommates. He sleeps downstairs on the couch and me and the kids sleep upstairs. I still try to tell him we need to get more romantic, but he is still ignoring me, when it comes to this situation. I also still question him a lot. Every time I lay down at night and I know that he is downstairs on his phone, not thinking about holding me or having a conversation with me, I know something is going on. All I can think about is him cheating on me with another female and it is making my mind go crazy. I know that this is not a healthy relationship, but I just don't know how to let go.

    I also still feel like a single mother, because I take on all the full responsibilities of the baby, even though we are living together. Denzel will probably hold the baby for 30 minutes in the morning, before he goes to work. Then, when he gets back home, he just goes about his business. Whenever the baby cries, he hands him back to me. If the baby poops, he hands him back to me. When the baby gets up, every two hours, I am the one having to wake up every time. I never get a break. I thought he would be a little more supportive, but I guess I thought a lot of things about him.

Chapter Twenty-Seven

Left And Stressed

Ever since I had the baby, I had to close my daycare, until the doctor approves me to work again. I knew this ahead of time, so Denzel and I talked and I told him he is going to have to help more with the bills. This is my house that we are living in, so I have been paying all the bills. But, I don't have any income and I need him now and he knows this.

I just got the gas and electric bill in the mail and it is $215 that I do not have. Denzel just got from work and I know he just got paid, so I'm going to talk to him about it. "Denzel, can you pay the energy bill, its $215." He pauses for a minute, then said, "No I'm broke." "How are you broke and you just got paid yesterday, where is your money at?" I said confused. "Don't worry about where my money at. I said I don't have it."

Is he serious right now?! He just got paid yesterday and he worked at least 40 hours. How can he say he has no money, he hasn't paid a bill yet? How can he live in this house and not help with this bill? He doesn't even care if the electricity gets paid? What is wrong with him? I'm not worried about anything. I'm going to do what I must do, to get my bills paid.

I'm still disappointed about what happened yesterday, I just don't understand how you don't feel the need to help with the bills. Now, he went to work in my car and he hasn't been back home all day. It's going on nine o'clock, when he got off work at four in the evening. Let me call him and see where he is at. Where are you?" I said. "I'm at this football game at Jefferson High School," he said with an attitude. Did he forget that he is driving my car and he did not even let me know he was taking my car anywhere, while I am at home with the baby all day? "Bring me my car," I said furiously.

He took no longer than ten minutes and he was at the house. He walked in with a mischievous look on his face. He sat down and said words that I never would have thought would come out of his mouth. "You know what, this just isn't working out. I think that we should just both co-parent. It would be best for our son." My heart quickly sank to my stomach, it felt as if the world had been crashing down right before me. "Co-parent, what do you mean co-parent?" I said. "I don't like the way you keep questioning me about everything I'm doing and then I don't like how you just told me to bring me your car." "So, you're leaving me with your son, because of that? The baby isn't even 6 weeks yet and you are going to leave us?" "I will never leave my son, but I have to leave this relationship."

Wow, this man begged me to have his child for so long and now that he is here, he is just going to leave me. I am so angry that I had a child with him. "I don't know what female got your mind all messed up, but I hope she is worth it." I am pissed off, I began to curse him out and I haven't cursed in about four years. I just couldn't believe he was leaving me and I just had the baby. Is it because you didn't want to pay no bills? Is that why you are leaving? I just don't understand, he is leaving me at the time when

I needed him the most. He was supposed to hold the house down, while I wasn't working, but now he is abandoning us.

He had this smirk on his face, like he just wanted to break me. He was smiling and laughing, while I was broken hearted and crying. I just never thought another man would leave me to raise another baby alone. There was a difference with Terrell. We were young and he never wanted a child. But, Denzel wanted this baby so bad and he begged me daily to get pregnant. Why would you want someone to have your child, if you aren't going to be with them?

He grabbed the baby and gave him a kiss and said, "I'll see you soon man, daddy love you." I couldn't stop the tears from falling down my face. He gave the baby back to me and said, "I'll be back to get my stuff soon." He threw me my keys and walked out the door. I'm going to be left alone, again, to raise another child. This is why I never wanted another child, until I got married. I wish I would have stuck with my first thought.

It's been a couple of weeks, since Denzel left and I have been dealing with everything just fine. I had to go down to social services and ask for help with my utility bills and help with my financial needs, since I won't be getting another check for about two months. One thing about me is I am not ashamed to ask for help, sometimes you need help to get back on your feet. But, it has been hard dealing with a new born baby, all by myself. I am sleep deprived and Denzel doesn't see the baby at all. All he does is ask me to send him pictures of him. I also asked him to get him some fall clothes, because he doesn't have any. But, he is acting like he can't do that either. I have no money at all and it is just hurting me to know that my son's father has a good job, lives no more than 5 miles away from us and he isn't helping with anything. It really hurts and people wonder why women can be so bitter. It's because we get put in difficult situations, where we should have never been in. No woman should have to raise a child alone. It is hard and it really makes you feel like you and your children have been abandoned.

Chapter Twenty-Eight

Reap What You Sow

Girl, I think that this is Denzel in this video. Go look at it on the internet. My home girl just wrote me this in my inbox. So, I went to where she told me to look, to watch the video and it is 100% Denzel in this video. What was he doing? Something that I would have never expected him to do. It was a video of him in the club dancing with some dark skinned, skinny girl, with booty shorts on. If you don't know what they are, they are short shorts that have your booty hanging out. As the girl began to shake her behind on him, he began to bend over and start licking her butt, like a wild animal. He was licking it for about 2 minutes straight, while all his friends were trying to pull him off, but he kept going at it. I just couldn't believe my eyes.

After I watched the video, I decided to let him know about this video of him, just in case he did not know that someone in the club was recording him. I began to video chat him and he picked up and said, "What's going on?" So, I replied, "Did you go to the club last night?" He huffed and said, "No." I said, "You don't have to lie to me. I just wanted to let you know that there was a disturbing video of you on the internet right now on Facebook, so I think you should go and handle that." He looked shocked and said, "Okay, thank you."

Next thing I know, not even an hour later, that video went viral. Everyone was talking about him, dogging him out, and laughing at him. It was so sad. I know that he had to be embarrassed. I was sad for him, but I was also hurt. He left me and my son to go out and do nasty things with a woman. What makes it even worse, is that he wouldn't touch me at all. I just don't understand why. What also made it worse, is that people started putting me in it, because we just had a baby together. They would say I am the "booty eater baby mom." It's crazy how this man has hurt me so much, but I still care about him. How does he feel about everyone treating him so awful? Everyone was waiting for me to say something bad about him, but I didn't do any of that. Everyone was saying enough bad things about him. I just let him know that I still care about him and I hope he's okay, even though he is going through this tough time.

You know, everything happens for a reason and what is done in the dark, shall come to the light. How Denzel treated me was just wrong and look at what he must face now. I can't believe that video, it just shows his true characteristics. He never was, what he was claiming to be. He wanted to be out and have fun. He didn't want to be in the house with his family and stay faithful. He wanted to mess with different woman and do what he thinks is fun. But, I'm not mad at him. I am a firm believer that you reap what you sow and you can't treat others bad without it coming back to you. It may not come back on you immediately, but it will catch up to you one day.

My whole family had seen this video and I am so embarrassed. Now, I have to explain to everyone that we are not together and he can do whatever it is he wants to do. I know that my parents really feel sorry for me. No parent wants to see their children go through pain and heartache. But, I am strong and I know that I will get through this.

Chapter Twenty-Nine

Sacrifice

 It is getting so cold and my son doesn't have any winter clothes. I don't know what I am going to do. My aunt sent me clothes for him, when he was a newborn. But, now, he needs a whole new wardrobe. I keep asking Denzel and he has not gotten our son anything. He owes me money, but he still won't give it to me. I could buy the baby things, with the money he owes me. He keeps saying that he is broke. But, how are you broke working a full-time job, with no bills? I'm confused. Why isn't he helping me provide for this needs of this child? Lord, please help me, because I am trying to keep my faith that You will provide, but my baby still doesn't have anything.

 I have never been a person to steal or do things that could get me in trouble, but my baby needs some clothes. I know that God provides for the children, but my faith is not where it use to be. My sister works at a department store and she said that she will let me get some clothes and diapers, for the low. She will change the prices, so that I can afford to get what he needs and I am honestly considering do that. I'm going to ask Denzel one more time to buy the baby some of the things he needs and if he says no again, I just have to do what I have to do as a mother. I must provide for my child, by any means necessary.

"Denzel, do you have the money you owe me, so that I can get the baby some winter clothes?" "No, I don't have any money. I don't have it. When I get it, I will give it to you." "What you mean you don't have it, when you just got paid today?" I said. "Yo, stop calling me, asking me for money." He hung up the phone on me. I can't believe he said stop asking him for money, like it isn't my money. Wow, how can he get upset, because his son needs clothes? Did he just hang up on me? Tears just began to flow, heavily, down my face. "What's wrong?" my mom said, feeling concerned. "Denzel won't help me get anything for the baby. I hate him. I swear I hate him," I cried harder and harder. My mom just embraced me and said, "It is going to be okay. God will provide for you and your children." I believed her, but my faith is weak and it is too cold for my son not to have any clothes to wear.

It just made me think about when Terrell would hang up on me, when I would tell him that our daughter needed things. How can these men not care about the needs of their own flesh and blood? I just can't believe I am going through the same thing I was going through 5 years ago, but with a different person. If I wanted to go through the same thing, I would have stayed with Terrell. I never would have thought, in a million years, that Denzel would have turned out to be just like Terrell.

I went and got everything that my kids need and my sister lowered the price of everything, so that I can afford it. I usually would never do anything that wasn't morally right, but I just couldn't go another day without my son having the things that he needs. I just hope that the Lord will forgive me for what I just did.

Chapter Thirty

Back Again

"My birthday this week, can you braid my hair Shay?" I really don't even want to see Denzel's face, but then again, I do want him to come and spend some time with the baby. "Okay, come over." I said.

He came walking in the house, looking like he's living good. He has a new outfit on and some brand-new Construction Timberland boots on. I can't believe this man is wearing new things, but he acts like he doesn't have any money to buy his son some clothes. I am trying to hold my tongue and just braid his hair and let him go back to wherever he is staying now. I don't even want to start nothing.

I began to braid Denzel's hair and I was kind of doing a good job, until we heard someone quietly knocking at the door. Denzel and I looked at each other in confusion, wondering who could it be knocking, this late? Denzel rushed up and looked out the door and out of nowhere he just began to put on his sneakers and coat back on. "Greg Diss is back, he just ran I'm about to go and catch him." He hopped in the car and went looking for him. I can't believe this man came back to my house again. I thought this was over. Now what am I going to do? I don't want to live in fear again and I don't want my children to be in danger.

Denzel just got back and he couldn't find that man anywhere. "Shay, I'm not going to let you and the kids stay here alone, with this man coming to the house. I'm going to stay here with you," Denzel said with sincerity. Okay, I would feel safe if you stayed here with us. He doesn't even know how much that meant to me. I am thankful that he can be here with us and help me more with the baby.

Let's make sure we get this straight first. We are not together, but we can stay together for right now. You can sleep downstairs and we will sleep upstairs. I appreciate you for protecting us.

Even though me and Denzel aren't together, seeing him every day is bothering me. All I keep thinking about is everything that he has done to me. I was trying to be nice to him and let him drive my car to work, while I'm at home with the baby. But, in my mind, I think he is just being sneaky and going to see females in my car. I'm happy that he is here for protection, but being around him is still messing with my mind. I can be happy one second with him, then, I think about all the girls he cheated on me with and how he hasn't helped me financially with the baby. Then, I just start being mean again. I really want to get away from him. I just wish I could move out of this house, so that I can have a fresh start without having a stalker. The other night we were pulling into the driveway and we seen Greg Diss running out of my garage, he has been hiding in there. Lord, I need to move now!

Chapter Thirty-One

Life Will Get Better

I must hurry up and call my landlord to let her know I had another baby, let me do that now. "Hey Sarah, this is Shay calling, I just wanted to inform you that I had another child, a baby boy!" "Congratulations, so you have two children now?" "Yes, I do," I said. "Well, that is perfect. I have a 3-bedroom, full house just for you, if you want it. I am fixing it up right now and you can move into it once we are done," she said. "I would love to move into the house Sarah." "Okay, I will give you a call, when it is ready for you to move in."

I know that the Lord hears my prayers. My landlord knew what I was going through, living in this house and I am so thankful that she is allowing me to move into one of her whole houses. She could have given anyone else this house, but she chose me and I know that it is because of the Lord's blessings. The Lord knows that if I move, I don't have to worry about needing a man to live with me, because I am afraid. I just want to get back right, fully with God and start going back to church. I know that this transition will be something that will be beneficial for my life.

How am I going to tell Denzel that I am moving? I don't want to tell him that he cannot come. I would feel like I was just using him to live with me, because of the man that was stalking me. But, I also really don't want him to come to my new house, because I will just be carrying extra baggage that I am trying to leave at my old house. I don't want to bring old problems into new situations. I want this house to be filled with joy, laughter, peace and God's presence. I want my children to be happy and to see their mother happy, for once. I don't want them to see the mother that is always arguing with her boyfriend, because he keeps cheating or he isn't helping enough. I want to provide a stable home for my children to grow up in and I know that if he comes along, nothing will change.

I don't want Denzel to feel upset about anything, so I am just going to ask him if he wants to come. If he says yes, then there will be a lot of changes, for him to stay there. If he says no, then I will feel relieved in a sense. I can have some peace, without my mind being stuck on him.

"Denzel, I'm supposed to be moving soon, are you coming with us?" He looked shocked, not knowing where and how. "Where are, you moving to?" "I am moving to the Southside of Rochester." "No, I'm good, I don't like it over there. Why are you trying to move, anyways?" "Denzel, you already know why I am moving. Why would I stay here and I have a stalker?" "Shay, I'm here to protect you now." "Denzel, you can get up and leave us at any time like, you been doing. I can't depend on you to stay and protect us," I said. "So, you really going to move?" he said. "Yes, I am going to move. God is blessing me with this house and I am going to move there." "How you know God is blessing you, not in that area?" he said. See, I can't deal with a naysayer. If I said that something is a blessing from God, why be skeptical? The only reason why he doesn't want us to move, is because he knows that I won't be dependent on him to protect us anymore. I'm moving regardless, if he likes it or not.

Chapter Thirty-Two

Leaving The Past Behind

Today is the day, I just got the call from my landlord saying I can pick up the keys to the house. I went and picked the keys up so fast! I pulled up to the house and it is everything that I wanted. It's on a quiet street and it has a gated back yard. I put the key in, opened the door and it was beautiful inside. Brand new, three bedrooms, 1 ½ bath, full house. It has brand new, beautiful carpet, brand new wooden floor in the kitchen and clean kitchen appliances included. I couldn't ask for anything better. I am so thankful that I am blessed to be in a new home.

I began to think about all the disturbing events that took place, while living in my other house. I have spent 3 years being stalked and tormented by this man Greg Diss. I remember having to lock my daughter and I in the room, while we slept at night, because we were both afraid that Greg Diss was going to get in. I remember the nights that I would stay up all night, crying and asking God why is this happening to me? Then, I began to think about the time when I use to stay up all night waiting on Denzel to come home, but he was out cheating. I thought about the times I would drop out of college because of being in deep depression.

I began to think about the times when me and Denzel would argue and he would leave me in an instant. Then, after he would leave me I would become fearful all over again, thinking that Greg Diss will be coming again. I remember the night Denzel and I argued, because I said that I didn't deserve to be treated the way he treats me. So, he said, "If you don't deserve the bad, then you don't deserve the good either." So, he went through my whole house and started ripping up everything he has ever bought me. He took the microwave, vacuum cleaner, iron, pictures, pillows and me and my daughter's sneakers. Whatever he bought, he took and threw it all on my front lawn.

All I can remember is all the bad things that took place in that home. I remember being so controlled in that relationship, if I smiled at another man or waved too hard at a man I know, he would curse me out and say that I must have slept with him. I couldn't wear certain clothes that were too tight or he would rip them up. He ripped up all my diaries and journals that I had since I was a little girl because it had other men names in them. He didn't want me wearing makeup, so I listened and did everything he said because I didn't want to be left alone in that house. I felt that I needed him to survive while living there but I'm just so happy I can now remove myself from that bad relationship. There are so many bad memorizes that I can recall, living there. I forgave him for all he did, I'm just ready to move on with my life. I am just so thankful that it is all over now.

Chapter Thirty-Three

Life Better Than Ever

Now that I have moved, I am now focused on me and my children and getting us closer to the Lord. Since I am in a new house, it is a new beginning and I have taken the time to focus on being a better woman. I have also been able to accomplish my main goal of graduating college. I finished my degree in Entrepreneurship and Applied Business with a GPA above a 3.0. I still remember the day when God told me to quit my job, while I focus on school and he will provide for me. God really did everything He ever told me He was going to do. I am so thankful. Going to school full-time and raising my children alone has been a challenge. But, you never know how strong you are, until you are put through challenges.

I also ended up getting some counseling and talked to a professional about the day that my virginity was taken. One day, I just broke down and had a panic attack. When I tried to talk to about it, I knew then that I needed some professional help and I must deal with the things of my past I never confronted. I finally dealt with what happened and admitted the truth. It funny how we can go through something so traumatic and be in denial for years, but one day that same thing will come back up again and you must face the truth of what happened to you. I faced my truth, it took me 8 years to admit what really happened and accept the truth. I talked to Terrell and I told him that I forgave him for what he did to me that night. I never realized that what happened, when I was 17 years old, really affected my life for years.

    I always wondered why intercourse felt so uncomfortable for me. I never knew why until I went to see a professional. They gave me so many answers to the questions I wondered about for years. Why did I stay with this man after what he did to me? Why was I often afraid to be alone with men? I even talked to the counselor about being stalked for three years and how that made me fear men even more. I finally dealt with my past and I can now move on with my future. Sometimes, you must get some professional help to get you through those traumatic experiences.

    My mind is clear and I'm focused on accomplishing many more things to come. The main thing that I must do, while I am at peace with myself and the Lord, is finish the book that He told me to write five years ago, called, "Journey of a Single Mother." I will never forget Him whispering those words to me and telling me to write the book. No matter how hard life may have been, I know why I had to go through the things I went through! When life tried to throw things at me to break me down, I prevailed. My troubles weren't in vain, I gain strength and wisdom and I can now help someone else get through those same things I once was struggling with. Life may not always go as planned, but always remember that God has the final plan for your life!

How to contact the Author

Dasharra Bridges is the CEO and Founder of JOASM! She is an actress and producer of the short film "Journey Of A Single Mother." She is the mother of two children and resides in the city of Rochester, NY.

Did you enjoy reading this book? Do you have any questions you would like answered? Maybe you are going through one of the same situations in the book and you need help getting through it. Maybe you just want to know what happened next, more of the story, more details. Guess what! You now have the chance to do these things. Dasharra Bridges will be having a book signing tour! At this book signing event, it will not only be a dinner but there will be an open forum where you can ask her anything and she will answer each question, honestly. If you would like to get tickets for this event, check to see if she is coming to a city near you, please visit: **dasharrabridges.com**.

Now that you read this book you are officially apart of JOASM! JOASM is a representation of strength we are simply Overcomer's that prevail through every obstacle!

Would you like to be featured on our page? Post a picture of you with this book to your social media with the hashtag #JOASM and check our page to see if you have been chosen!

Email for Booking: joasmtm@gmail.com

Keep in touch!

Follow Me:
facebook.com/dasharra.bridges
instagram.com/iamdasharra
twitter.com/iamdasharra

Dasharra Bridges